Hadrian's Wall

A Teacher's Handbook

David Walmsley

Contents

Historical background	2
What is Hadrian's Wall?	4
Constructing the Wall	8
Life in the forts	9
Religion on the Wall	10
Description of the sites	
Housesteads Fort	11
Chesters Fort	14
Corbridge Town	17
South Shields Fort	20
Wallsend Fort	20
Birdoswald Fort	21
Vindolanda	21
Resource sheets	
Where did the Romans come from?	22
Building the Wall	23
Building the forts	24
Conquest and departure	26
Educational approaches	28
Scheme of work	30
Housesteads Fort	32
Corbridge Town	34
Chesters Fort	36
Role-play activities	38
Language and literacy	39
Bibliography and resources	40

An artist's impression of how the wall at Walltown Crags might have looked.

Historical background

Julius Caesar led two expeditions to Britain, in 55 BC and again in 54 BC in order to establish links with Rome. However, after a build up of hostilities between Britain and Rome, the Emperor Claudius instigated a full-scale invasion in AD 43. The suppression of Britain was then continued under Agricola, who led a major invasion into Scotland and routed the Celts at the Battle of Mons Graupius in AD 84. However, after his recall to Rome, the occupying forces were unable to maintain their hold over Scotland and eventually withdrew south. The frontier then became a patrolled road, known as the Stanegate, which linked a series of forts and watchtowers, and stretched from the Tyne to the Solway.

About AD 117 there seems to have been major unrest amongst British tribes and in AD 122 when the Emperor Hadrian visited Britain he decided to replace the Stanegate with a more physical barrier to control the frontier. This was to take the form of a wall, and was built approximately two miles north of the Stanegate, across one of the narrowest parts of Britain. It was built by three legions, legio II Augusta, legio VI Victrix and legio XX Valeria Victrix. What purpose Hadrian intended the Wall to fulfil is still the cause of much speculation, but in practical terms it provided:

■ a defensible barrier to repel invasions and marauding tribesmen

■ a convenient customs point to levy taxes on goods leaving and entering Roman Britain

■ a method to control communication between hostile tribes north and south of the Wall

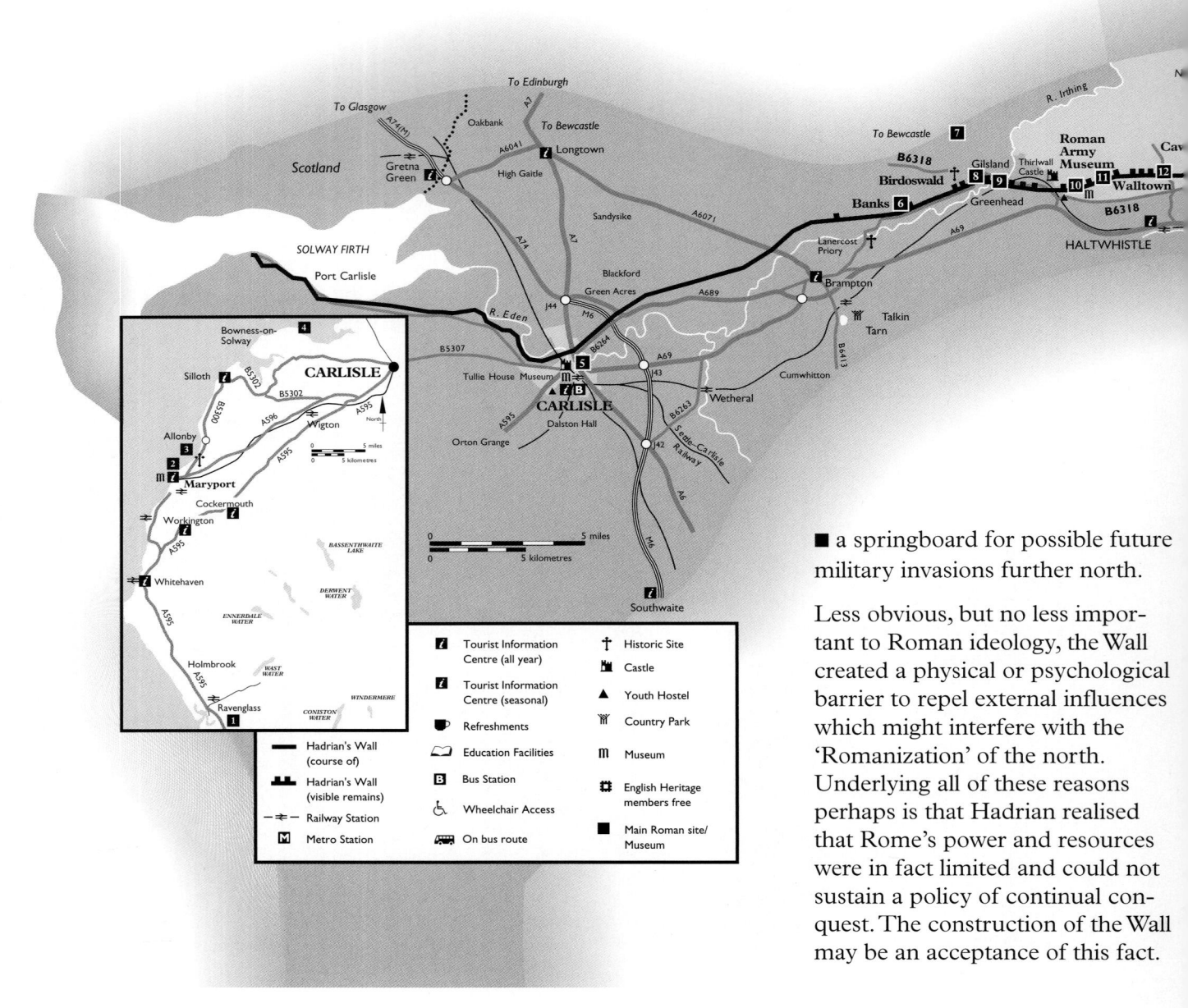

■ a springboard for possible future military invasions further north.

Less obvious, but no less important to Roman ideology, the Wall created a physical or psychological barrier to repel external influences which might interfere with the 'Romanization' of the north. Underlying all of these reasons perhaps is that Hadrian realised that Rome's power and resources were in fact limited and could not sustain a policy of continual conquest. The construction of the Wall may be an acceptance of this fact.

The Wall, however, was only one component of the frontier system, which evolved over a number of years. The frontier also consisted of milecastles and turrets, and while the Wall was under construction it was decided to build a series of large forts along its line. All these structures were to be protected to the north by a ditch and to the south by the vallum, which created a military zone with restricted access. Roads and bridges were built to ensure the swift deployment of men, the transport of supplies and to improve communications. Through time civilian settlements also grew up to the south of the forts.

Hadrian was succeeded by Antoninus Pius, and Imperial policy changed. New attempts were made to conquer Scotland, and within a short time the southern part of the country came under Roman control again. A new frontier, a turf wall known as the Antonine Wall, was built nearly 100 miles north of Hadrian's Wall across a narrow neck of Scotland between the Firth of Forth and the Firth of Clyde. This was half the length of Hadrian's Wall and should have been a more effective and economical barrier, but it eventually needed to be defended by up to 26 forts. It too had a number of milecastles along its length and became one of the most heavily defended frontiers in the Roman Empire.

However by about AD 158 the Antonine Wall was abandoned and Hadrian's Wall was reinstated as the frontier. The army later reoccupied the Antonine Wall for a further few years before withdrawing permanently to Hadrian's Wall.

During the next 250 years there were a number of changes to the Wall and its defences. Some were the result of amendments to its design, repairs to its structures or improvements in its operation. Others were a direct consequence of a change in Roman policy and reorganisation within the army.

In the late fourth century and early fifth century civil wars, revolts in other parts of the Empire and an invasion by Germanic tribes, who sacked Rome in AD 410 resulted in large parts of the army being recalled from Britain.

The end of Roman Britain is traditionally set at AD 410 when Emperor Honorius sent a letter to the cities of Britain informing them that in future they would have to defend themselves against attack and could not rely on the Roman army for support. Any soldiers remaining on Hadrian's Wall would by then have been native born and probably lived with their families inside the forts. When the army ceased to pay the British soldiers these men probably remained at the forts but devoted more time to farming which would then have become their livelihood.

Slowly, the forts were abandoned and new settlers established their own settlements. The Wall and its structures then became a convenient source of building stone for homes, farms, churches and castles. Its stone was even used to construct a road to enable troops to move quickly between Newcastle and Carlisle after the 1745 Jacobite Rebellion. This road, now the B6318, is known locally as the 'Military Road' (not to be confused with the Roman 'military way' which is the road connecting the forts).

Fortunately, in the more remote areas stretches of the Wall and some of its military structures have survived.

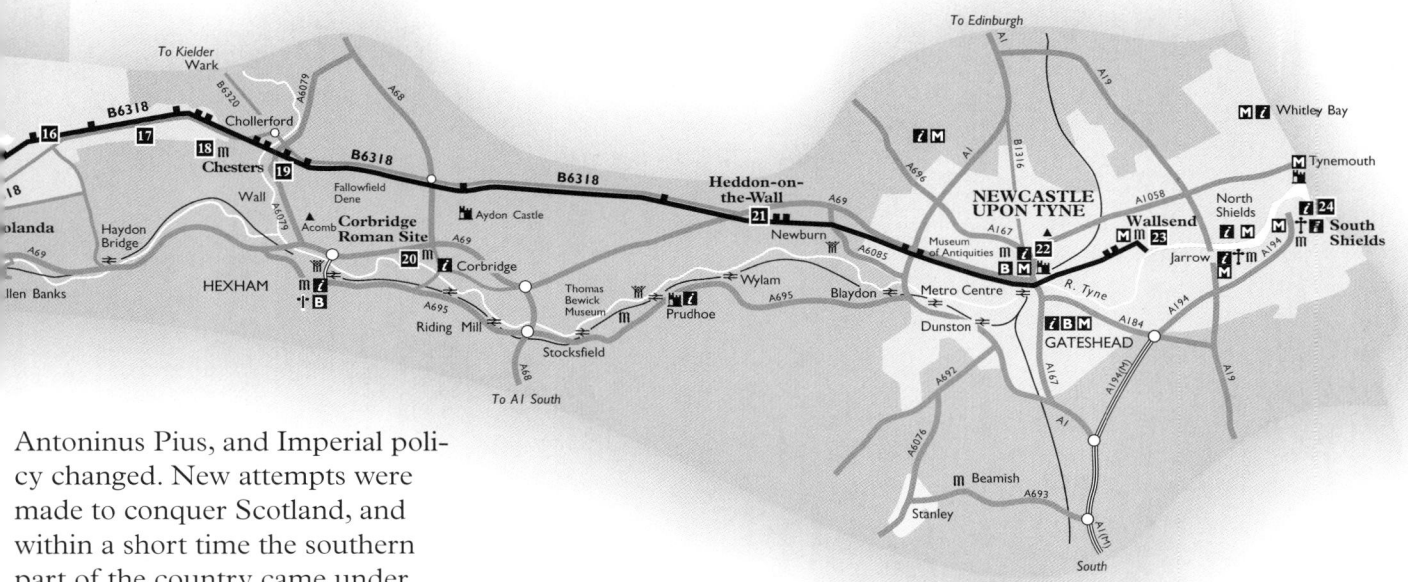

Today, Hadrian's Wall is a significant tourist attraction, and its importance was realised by UNESCO in 1987 when it was inscribed on the list of world heritage sites.

What is Hadrian's Wall?

Section of the Narrow Wall at Planetrees built on foundations intended for the Broad Wall.

The Wall

This was originally planned to be 76 Roman miles long (about 111km) running from Newcastle to Bowness-on-Solway on higher ground to the north of the Stanegate. It was later extended to Wallsend to make a total length of 80 Roman miles. The Wall was not built by starting from one end, but stretches were constructed simultaneously. The three legions who constructed the Wall divided the work up into 8-10km sections. The eastern part of the Wall (from Newcastle to the River Irthing) was built of stone from the beginning. Its intended line was marked out by a foundation layer 10 Roman feet (3m) wide and at those places where it was subsequently built to its intended thickness it became known as the Broad Wall.

However once it was decided to construct forts along the Wall, the remaining sections were completed to a narrower width and are known as the Narrow Wall.

The western part of the Wall (from the River Irthing to Bowness) was originally built of turf, often on a cobbled base up to 6m wide. Within about ten years the Turf Wall was rebuilt in stone, and on a slightly different line. Archaeological evidence suggests that the height of the stone wall was between 3.5 and 4m, and the Turf Wall was probably about 3.6m high. There is only slight evidence that there was a walk and a parapet along the top of the Wall. If the army did patrol the top of the Wall, vast numbers of soldiers would have been needed just to keep watch, leaving little time for other duties. Recent excavations also suggest that the face of the wall was not left as bare stone. At Castle Nick (west of Housesteads) it had been whitewashed and at Denton (near Newcastle) it was rendered with mortar. This must have had the effect of making the Wall stand out very clearly in the landscape.

Ditch

This was usually 8-12m wide and 2.7-3m deep and was dug close to the northern face of the Wall except where the Wall is built on a cliff edge. It was intended to prevent anyone charging at the Wall. The fact that the Wall and it's forts were protected on both sides - to the north by the ditch and to the south by the Vallum - indicates that the Wall did not necessarily divide friendly tribes from hostile ones.

Turf Wall. Built in courses of turves, each measuring 45x30x15cm.

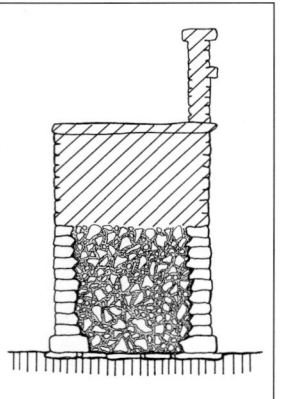

Broad Wall. The facing stones are set in lime mortar and the rubble core is set in puddled clay.

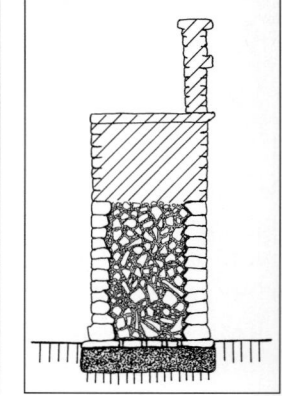

Narrow Wall. Both the facing stones and rubble core are set in lime mortar. The foundations are of clay and cobble.

Below: Cross-section of the frontier zone.

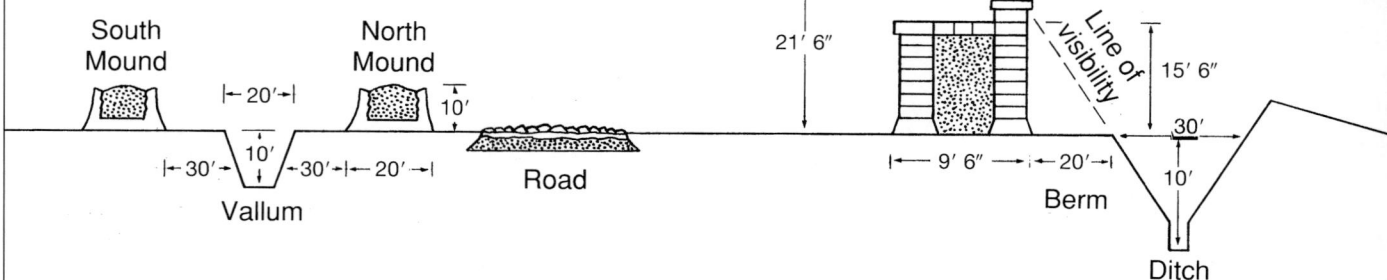

Vallum

The Vallum was not part of the original plan but was constructed to the south of the Wall whilst building work was in progress. It was a broad, flat-bottomed ditch with a bank on either side, and protected the frontier zone from attack from behind. In some places the Vallum runs close to the Wall; elsewhere it lies up to 1km away. Crossing points were made to provide access to the forts.

To assist with communication along the Wall a road was later built along the line of the Vallum and is now known as the 'military way'.

Benwell Vallum crossing as it may have appeared shortly after its construction. Note the different sizes of stone used and the building inscription above.

Milecastles

These small Roman forts were built against the Wall at intervals of one Roman mile (1.6km) regardless of geographical conditions. Built to a standard plan with one or two long buildings of timber or stone inside, they provided accommodation for up to 8 - 32 men.

Prior to the building of the Wall forts the milecastles were intended to provide the main accommodation for soldiers patrolling the Wall. They were the only means for native people to cross the Wall and therefore provided a convenient point to levy a tax on goods passing through, and to control movement across the frontier.

The Wall and Vallum at Cawfields. Cutting through the landscape behind the Wall the Vallum protected the southern approaches to the Wall zone.

Remains of milecastle 42 at Cawfields.

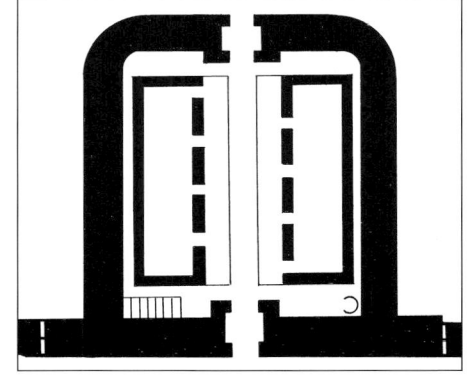

Below: Artist's impression of a typical milecastle.

Typical layout of a milecastle.

Turrets

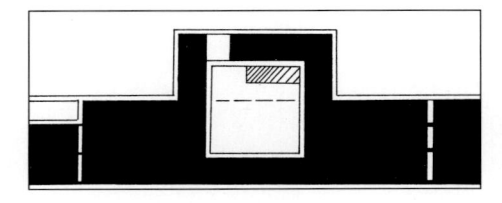

Between each milecastle were two evenly spaced small turrets. They were built at the same time as the foundations of the Wall. All turrets, including those along the Turf Wall, were built of stone. They were very basic and were intended for temporary occupation by probably no more than twelve men. Presumably higher than the Wall itself, they may have been used as lookout posts or for signalling messages along the wall (some of the signal towers which had earlier been built to guard the Stanegate were also amalgamated into the defences along the Wall). Each turret or milecastle was within sight of its neighbour, thereby affording mutual protection whilst ensuring total surveillance and speedy communication along the Wall. Little evidence remains to show what the top of the turrets would have looked like. In the centre of the floor was a hearth, used for keeping warm and cooking. Access to the upper floor and walkway was by a ladder.

The turrets are thought to have been built before the Wall. They were constructed with short sections of spur wall on either side in readiness for connection to the Wall once that section was built.

Denton Hall Turret.

The turrets were built to a standard design, but the upper levels are still open to speculation. Three different building styles are apparent, possibly due to the three legions who built the Wall.

Above: The western 48 km were originally built in turf. This illustration shows how a turret may have appeared on the Turf Wall. Pieces of glass found at some turrets suggest that the windows may have been glazed.

Bridges

The line of the Wall crosses three main rivers: the North Tyne at Chesters, the Irthing at Willowford, and the Eden near Carlisle. Archaeological evidence indicates that strong stone bridges carried the Wall across the Irthing and the North Tyne but little is known about the bridge which crossed the Eden. As a result of changes in the courses of the rivers at Chesters and Willowford the piers can be seen on dry land at the side of the river.

Outpost forts

Some distance to the north of the Wall were outpost forts such as those at Bewcastle, Netherby and Birrens. Soldiers here monitored the local situation and fed information back to the army stationed on the Wall, perhaps using a chain of signalling beacons. Later, the Wall garrison was also given advanced warning by more outpost forts built along the main roads north.

West coast defences

Military defences continued beyond the western end of the Wall down the Cumbrian coast for a further 26 miles by means of a series of milefortlets and watchtowers. Similar in design to those on the Wall, they were also spaced respectively at intervals of one mile and a third of a mile. The towers were built of stone and the milefortlets of turf and timber. Unlike the Wall milecastles the milefortlets were never rebuilt in stone.

The forts

It was initially intended to base the soldiers manning the Wall at the Stanegate forts. However some were up to 2 miles (3km) away and this would have caused a delay in deploying troops to the Wall in times of emergency. So the plan was changed and eventually 16 forts were built along its line. The construction of the Wall was interrupted until these forts were built.

The standard plan of Roman forts, based upon that of marching camps, was used for the forts along the Wall. Their shape was rectangular with rounded corners - like a playing card - and would usually be one and a half times as long as broad. They were surrounded by at least one ditch. Each fort had a high curtain wall with towers at regular intervals and backed by earth ramparts. Against the ramparts were bakehouses and ovens, deliberately isolated from other buildings due to fire risk.

Access into the fort was through fortified gateways with double gates. Three of these usually led out onto the land beyond the Wall to allow troops and cavalry to move northwards quickly. Immediately inside the curtain wall was a perimeter road. Inside, the fort was divided into three areas with the most important buildings (headquarters building, the commanding officer's house, the granaries and hospital) in the middle, the safest part of the fort. At either end were the barracks, workshops and stables.

South of the forts, civilian settlements (vici) grew up. Initially these were temporary buildings but through time they became more established and were replaced in stone. A vicus usually contained a bathhouse, temples, lodging houses, shops, inns, workshops and domestic accommodation.

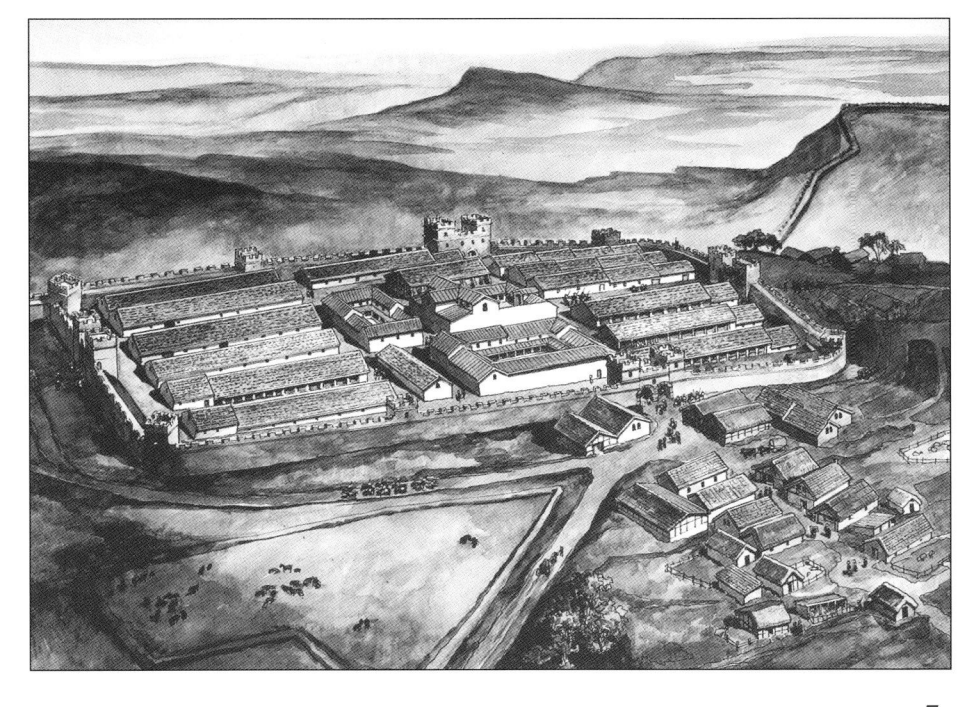

Artist's impression of the Roman bridge at Chesters.

Artist's impression of Housesteads Fort.

Constructing the Wall

The Wall was built in short sections by working parties from the regular Roman army (legionaries).

The materials required for building the Wall and its associated structures were:

- stone for facing the Wall and other structures
- rubble for the core of the Wall
- clay for the foundations and for mixing with the core. It was also used to make tiles for roofs, floors and hypocausts
- limestone to make mortar
- cut turves for the Turf Wall and its milecastles
- water to mix the mortar
- timber for the gates, roofs, buildings and scaffolding, for fuel and for burning lime
- iron for locks, hinges and tools
- lead for water pipes and for setting iron clamps and iron hinge collars into stones.

Most of these materials were available locally although some, for example iron and lead, were brought from elsewhere in Britain. The Wall was faced with carefully shaped square or rectangular blocks of sandstone. In the west some had to be brought from quarries across the Solway Firth. In the east some of the stone may have been ferried along the River Tyne from further afield.

In the central section of the Wall, basalt, which forms the underlying Whin Sill, was not generally used as facing stone because it was too hard for stonemasons to cut into regular shapes.

The rubble core consisted of any available stone which was set in clay and capped with mortar. Though later when sections of the Wall needed rebuilding they were set almost entirely in mortar.

Lime for mortar was produced from limestone quarried near the Wall. It was burnt with charcoal in limekilns and then mixed with sand, gravel and water to produce mortar. This mortar set very hard and was resistant to water and weather. The remains of limekilns can be seen at numerous points on either side of the 'Military Road'.

Timber would have been readily available since in Roman times the area was probably more heavily forested, particularly on the lower lying land and in the river valleys.

Building inscriptions were incorporated into structures to record work completed by each unit. These inscriptions have helped archaeologists determine when parts of the Wall were built and by whom.

The Vallum was built in lengths of about 100 yds (91.4 ms). When each section was complete two inscriptions on opposite sides of the Vallum were installed by the soldiers who built it.

The buildings within the forts were also built by legionaries. Each legion contained skilled engineers, surveyors, masons, carpenters and smiths.

Life in the forts

An ordinary soldier, having completed his training, was likely to spend only a small proportion of his time in combat. Evidence suggests that considerable numbers of soldiers could be on detachment, with up to two-thirds of the total force at various places including Corbridge, London, or as part of the governor's guard. Also many soldiers may have been on sick leave, but much of their time was probably spent in the following ways:

■ training - daily practice on the parade ground outside the fort; practice in digging ditches for marching camps (overnight camp constructed when the army was on campaign); mock attacks; weapons drill

■ guard duty - in the headquarters building; at the gates of forts; at one of the milecastles and turrets

■ duties - cleaning the latrines and the bathhouse; fetching fuel for the bathhouse; cleaning his own equipment and the equipment of his superiors; gathering fodder for the animals; cooking fuel for his barrack block

■ patrol duty - long periods would be spent patrolling areas north and south of the Wall or protecting supplies in transit

■ leave - there was some provision for soldiers to have leave from the fort where they were stationed. Many would have visited nearby towns such as Corbridge

■ free time - could be spent in the baths which were pleasantly warm, especially in winter, or in the shops and inns in the settlements outside most forts. Hunting and gambling would have been popular pursuits. The museum at Chesters shows spurs which would have been used in cockfighting.

Before AD 197 soldiers were not allowed to marry. Many found unofficial wives (possibly married under local native law rather than Roman law) or girlfriends from the local tribes. Senior officers and centurions often travelled with their wives and families. By the time they were discharged after twenty-five years up to forty percent of soldiers were 'married'.

The commanding officer's wife and family would have lived with him in his large house inside the fort. The wives and girlfriends of ordinary soldiers would have lived in the settlements outside the fort.

Many units had a symbol. The boar was the emblem of the Twentieth Legion. The winged horse was the emblem of the Second Legion.

Evidence has been discovered to show that the soldiers enjoyed different forms of gambling and games.

Legionary issuing orders to an auxiliary on guard duty at a gateway.

Soldiers had a varied diet, eating bread, soup, meat, fish and vegetables, and drinking ale and wine. Inside a turret soldiers cooked over an open hearth near an open window. The upper floor was reached by a ladder resting on a stone platform.

Religion on the Wall

There was a great degree of religious tolerance in the Roman Empire. Units were allowed to worship the gods of their homeland, and we know that along the Wall, Dolichenus, a Syrian cult, and Attis, a Phrygian cult were worhipped. Mithraism, a cult which originated in the Middle East, was widely practised on the Wall and the remains of a temple to Mithras can be visited at Carrawburgh.

All soldiers however were expected to acknowledge and be loyal to the divine spirits of the dead emperors. A statue of the current emperor was always set up in the regimental shrine in the HQ building and the anniversaries of his birth, accession and victory days were celebrated. Statues and altars to gods important to the army were also set up in the shrine, especially Jupiter, Victory and Mars. Hadrian in his reorganisation of the Roman army added the worship of Discipulina, the god of discipline. Only these 'official' Roman gods, however, were permitted inside the actual fort.

In each province the native people were allowed to continue to worship their own gods, and amongst local gods worshipped on the Wall was Antenociticus. A temple dedicated to him can be seen at Benwell. Deities associated with rivers, streams and forests were worshipped, and outside the fort at Carrawburgh was a well sacred to Coventina (a water nymph). In it was discovered 10 altars, around 16,000 coins, and many other objects, all thrown in as offerings to the goddess.

The Romans were also very superstitious and often used good-luck charms. The phallus was frequently used: many examples were carved on the Wall itself or on buildings in the forts. One can be seen on a paving slab in the headquarters building at Chesters.

Evidence of religious worship can be found in all museums along the Wall, including small figures of household gods, statues from regimental shrines, bells and spoons used in rites of worship, and jewellery such as rings and brooches.

Statue of a river god.

Dedication to Coventina, a water nymph.

Decorative relief showing the sun god.

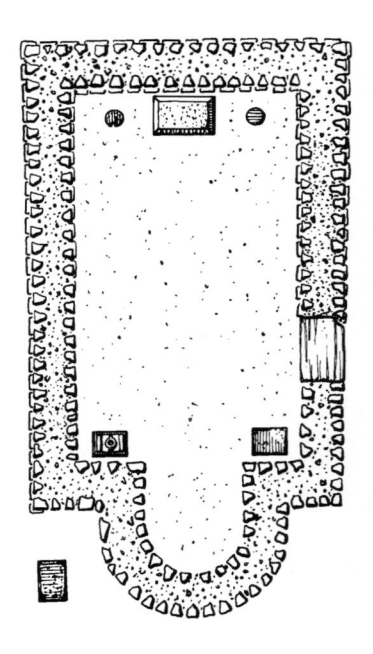

Temple of Mithras, Carrawburgh.

Plan of the temple at Benwell. This characteristic shape of a temple can also be seen at Corbridge.

Description of the sites

Housesteads Fort

Housesteads is situated high on a ridge with extensive views in all directions. It was occupied by the First Cohort of the Tungrians, an infantry regiment, which was intended to be 1000 strong.

A turret for the Wall had earlier been built on the site. This was dismantled when it was decided to build a fort here, but excavations have exposed its foundations. Around the south and east of the fort a civilian settlement developed. The water supply for the fort came from the Knag Burn, but it was supplemented by several tanks collecting rainwater and water from the roofs of buildings.

Gatehouses

The gatehouses of Roman forts were built to a standard plan with two arched entrances flanked by guard chambers and towers above.

The gateways of Roman forts followed a standard plan.

Being the most vulnerable part of the fort they were often constructed of massive square blocks of stone, whereas the rest of the fort's walls and towers were constructed with smaller blocks of stone.

The east gate was the main point of entry. Its southern passage was later blocked up, and the guard chamber was converted into a coal store, presumably for the new baths built nearby inside the fort.

The west gate is the best preserved as it was completely blocked shortly after the fort was built. Consequently features like its drawbar slots and the pivot holes for the gate's turning posts are visible.

The north gate ceased to be used by the end of the second century as successive resurfacing had raised the road level inside the fort so much that the approaches became too steep (these approaches were removed during excavations). The only way through Hadrian's Wall afterwards was the nearby Knag Burn gate. The east passage was soon blocked up and shows the original level of the road.

Against the south gate are the remains of a bastle house (fortified farmhouse). Later, a corn-drying kiln was built in the east tower of the gatehouse.

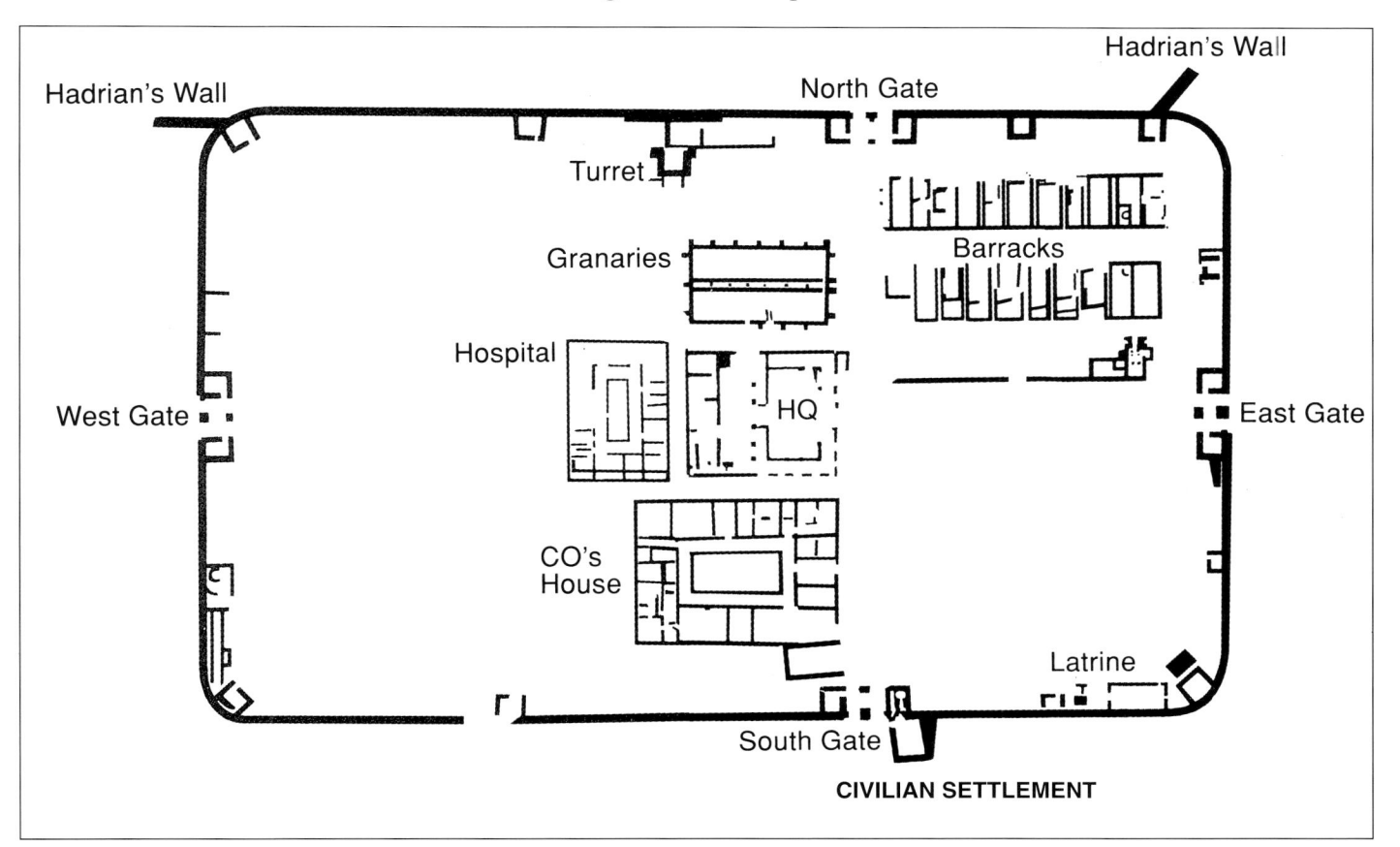

Most forts were built on a north-south axis with three gates opening onto territory to the north of the Wall. However at Housesteads the layout of the land necessitated building the fort on an east-west axis with only the north gate allowing access through the Wall.

Artist's impression of the granaries.

Granaries

The granaries were used to store foodstuffs, mainly grain, for daily use as well as reserve provisions for sieges or campaigns. They were originally one building, which was later divided into two. A row of six stone piers between the two central walls helped support the large roof when it was just one building. They had timber floors which were raised off the ground to provide a dry, vermin-free environment. The rows of stone supports and the joist holes for the floor timbers remain. The vents down the outer walls ensured the circulation of air which was necessary to keep grain dry. The granaries had a broad roof with a wide eavesdrip to channel rainwater away and keep the walls dry. Buttresses gave extra support to the heavy stone roof and prevented the walls from buckling outwards. The loading bays were on the west end because goods were brought in through the west gate to avoid interfering with the business in and around the headquarters building. As the garrison's size declined the north granary was no longer used and the south granary was subdivided by a cross wall, allowing part of it to be used as domestic accommodation. (The corn-drying kiln in the south granary is post Roman.)

Hospital

This was built around a central colonnaded courtyard and consists of a large room to the north, believed to be an operating theatre, and a series of small wards around the remaining three sides. There is a latrine in the south west corner with a drain leading off. The colonnade was later demolished and flagstones were laid in its place. As with other buildings in the fort, it too was converted to domestic use in the fourth century.

Headquarters building

This was the most important building as it was the seat of authority and the operations centre of the fort. It was divided into three sections; a courtyard, an assembly hall and a row of offices. The assembly hall had an aisle on its east side, now marked by a row of stone columns. In the north west corner is a raised platform where the commanding officer would address his troops, and at the south end of the hall is a raised stone base which would have been used for inscriptions or statues. On the east side of the hall are the large double doors with the pivot holes on the threshold.

The offices were used by the regimental clerks, but the middle room served as the shrine which housed the regimental standards, statues of the Emperor, and altars to various gods. Grooves on the stone floor show where there would have been a decorated screen. Below this would normally be a strongroom, as seen at Chesters and Corbridge, but the hardness of the rock made this impossible and a nearby room must have been used instead.

Around three sides of the courtyard was a colonnade. This was later filled in to create additional offices and hearths, perhaps for workshops, but the original column bases are still visible. In the north west corner are gutters in the stone paving, which carried much needed water to other parts of the fort. There was a sundial here (now in the museum at Chesters) which was used to regulate duty rosters.

A hospital for sick and injured soldiers was an integral part of the planning of many forts.

Commanding officer's house

This was the largest and most luxurious building in the fort, providing accommodation for the commanding officer, his family and personal staff. It is similar to the design of town houses throughout the Roman Empire, with a series of rooms around an open courtyard. The commanding officer and his family lived in rooms in the north and west ranges, many of which had under-floor heating and plastered walls. A room in the centre of the north range still has its hypocaust: it was originally a private bath, but was later used as a dining room. The supports of the hypocaust are made from single pieces of stone, recycled columns and stacks of flat stones. Channels in the walls held box flue tiles. At the east end of the north range was a kitchen with an oven. In the centre of the west range is a latrine. The east range contained rooms for servants, and a stable - the paved room with a tank at the south east corner.

Barrack blocks

These were initially long buildings divided into ten units, each housing eight soldiers. Each unit had a room at the front for storing equipment and a room at the back for sleeping. At the end of each block was more spacious accommodation for the centurion. In the early fourth century the barracks were replaced with rows of small chalet-style buildings, joined together by a rear wall. They may have become family homes when the garrison was reduced and the soldiers moved their families inside the fort for security reasons. Many rooms have flagged floors and hearths. A communal oven was later built into the eastern building of each row.

Nearby is a long, large building constructed of bigger blocks of stone, and with buttresses along its length. This was probably built in the third century as an imperial storehouse for the collection of taxes.

Individual living units.

Latrines

The latrines were housed in one large building, accommodating up to 30 men at any one time without any partitions. The building was probably open to the sky, but would have had a narrow sloping roof above the seats. It was built against the south wall of the fort where gravity was used to channel water through the drains and out through the base of the fort wall. The water came from rainwater, collected in a huge tank from the roof of the nearby angle tower. The hole at its base would have been plugged, releasing the water when necessary. The edge of the tank is worn, which was probably caused

Artist's impression of a barrack block in the second century.

Artist's impression of a barrack block in the fourth century.

The latrines at Housesteads. Providing pupils with artists' illustrations to use on site will help them understand the remaining evidence and pinpoint clues which have enabled the artist to create the picture.

by soldiers washing their clothes in it or sharpening their weapons on the stone. This tank was built of carefully jointed sandstone slabs, which were clamped together with iron inserts (some still in place). Molten lead was then poured over them to prevent the iron from rusting and to seal any gaps. A smaller tank to the west was also connected to this system. Additional water came from other parts of the fort via a network of stone channels. The narrow stone channel inside the building held running water to clean sponges (a forerunner of toilet tissue), and was supplemented by two stone troughs when the channel became too worn. The water in this channel flowed clockwise and downwards before emptying into the channel below the wooden seats to help flush the waste away.

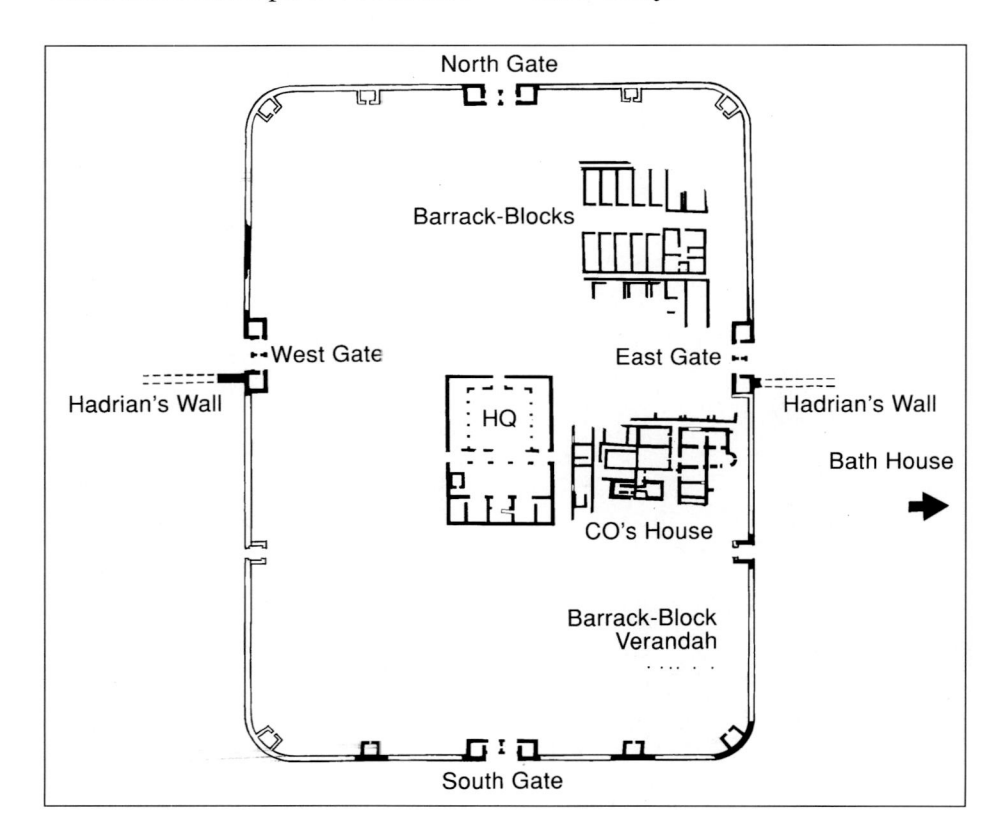

Vicus (civilian settlement)
Outside the south gate was a civilian settlement. This contained an inn, shops and workshops, and was where soldiers would spend their spare time. The buildings are mainly long and narrow, with the front part used for business and the rear part for accommodation. In one building, known as the 'murder' house, two buried skeletons were found, one with a knife fragment in his ribs. As burials were not permitted in Roman settlements, it is assumed that the man and woman were murdered and their bodies hidden.

Chesters Fort

This fort was built to guard a bridge that carried Hadrians's Wall and the military way over the River North Tyne. It housed a cavalry regiment, and from the end of the second century was the base for the Second Cavalry Regiment of Asturians. Like most forts, Chesters was built with three of its main gates opening on the north side of the Wall. Two extra, single-passage gates led onto the Military Way. As with other forts a civilian settlement (unexcavated) grew up to the south.

Gatehouses

All the main gateways and the additional east gate are visible. The main east and west gateways were later blocked up, leaving only the north gate to give access through the Wall.

Below the east passage of the **north gate** is a channel constructed of flat stones, supplying water to the fort.

The thresholds and stop-blocks for the gates of the **west gate** show little sign of wear, implying that the gateways were blocked up shortly after their construction. One of the iron collars holding the door pivots still remains. An underground channel supplied water to the north guard chamber, where a stone platform may have been the base of a water tank. Next to the north guard chamber are the remains of an oven.

The **south gate** shows much evidence of use; its numerous resurfacings raised the height of the roadway by a metre. Flat slabs cover a water channel, which may have come from the west gate and could have delivered water to the civilian settlement.

The **east gate** is one of the most impressive anywhere along the Wall with the height of one pier reaching to the beginning of the arch. As it led directly onto the river it would barely have been used and was soon blocked up. Attached to the south tower is a short stretch of Hadrian's Wall.

Barrack blocks

Two blocks face one another across a narrow road, which has a drain down its centre that would have been covered by stone slabs. At the end of each block is a suite of rooms for the centurion. Each barrack room would have accommodated eight soldiers, and was divided in two by a timber partition. The rear section was used for sleeping and the front for storing equipment. The rooms are slightly larger than those in other forts as Chesters housed a cavalry unit, whose men would have required extra storage space for their equipment and for their horses.

The east gate as it may have looked shortly after its construction. Hadrian's Wall joins it on the left.

Headquarters building

The headquarters building is situated in the middle of the fort and was the operations centre. It is divided into three sections: a courtyard, an assembly hall and a row of offices. The large paved courtyard has a colonnade around three sides. The guttering on the paving would have channelled rainwater from the roofs of the colonnade, and shows the extent of the overhanging roof. In the courtyard there is a well and nearby, a good-luck 'phallus' has been carved on one of the paving slabs.

The assembly hall was used for business, hearings and ceremonies. Against the west wall is the platform on which the commanding officer would address the troops.

Five small rooms lead off the hall. The middle room, separated by a screen from the assembly hall, housed the shrine which contained a statue of the emperor, the regimental standards and altars and statues to various gods. Because it was always guarded a strongroom was built below to store the soldiers' pay and savings. The long groove on the flagged floor marks the fixing for the screen. The other four rooms were used as offices for the regimental clerks for accounting and administrative purposes.

Commanding officer's house

This was the largest and most luxurious building in the fort, providing accommodation for the commanding officer, his family and personal staff. It was similar to the design of town houses throughout the Roman Empire, reflecting his status. The house had several rooms around three sides of a central courtyard. Additional rooms were added which filled much of the courtyard. Many of these rooms had underfloor heating with hypocausts constructed of roughly-shaped columns, courses of rectangular stones or square red tiles. The door thresholds show the level of the floor. A small private bathhouse was added later, and has a decorated moulded plinth unlike the more utilitarian stonework of earlier parts of this building.

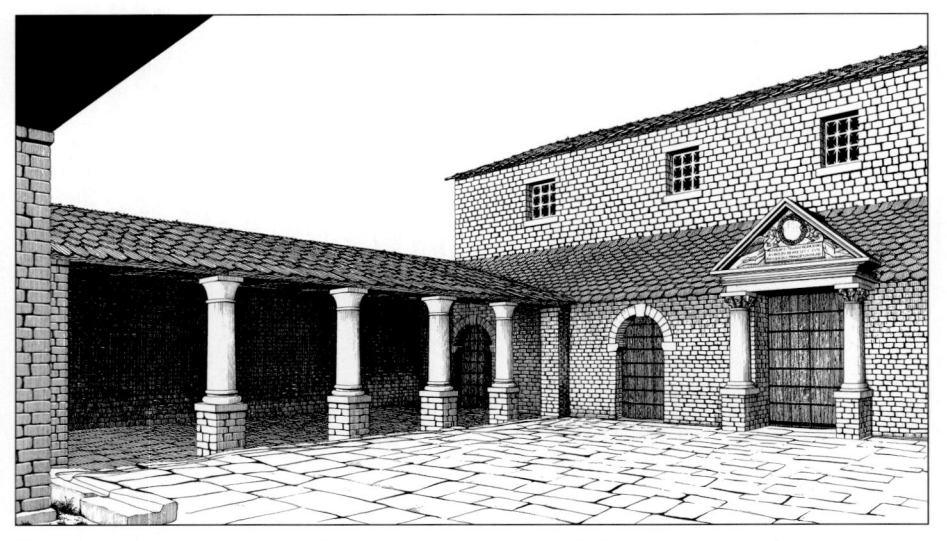

The courtyard and 'cross hall' of the headquarters building.

Artist's impression of the bathhouse at Chesters.

Plan of the bathhouse.

Bathhouse

The bathhouse was built outside the fort because of the risk of fire. It has a large changing room which would also have been used for exercising, socialising and even gambling. Along one wall are seven niches, but their function is uncertain. At its lower (riverside) end are the latrines. They consisted of deep channels between two walls, over which wooden seats were suspended. Their main source of water is uncertain but stone channels show that water was run off from the cold bath.

Beyond the changing room are the two rooms of the hot dry suite on the right, the cold bath and cold plunge on the left, and the warm and hot steam rooms straight ahead. Leading off the hot steam room is a D-shaped hot bath, where traces of plaster can be seen on the walls. The hot dry room has large stone door jambs because wood jambs would have warped in the extreme heat. Bathers probably wore thick wooden-soled shoes to avoid burning their feet.

To the south of the hot rooms is a platform which may have housed the boiler. The series of holes high in the walls may have been for pipes. Except for the changing room, all other rooms were supported on hypocausts. (The level that visitors are walking on is actually the ground below the hypocaust. The door thresholds indicate the level of the actual floor of the baths.)

Below the raised floor are the stoke holes for the three furnaces: they heat the warm rooms, the hot steam room and the hot dry room.

Corbridge Town

The settlement at Corbridge began as a fort to guard a crossing of the River Tyne and then later the junction of the Stanegate and Dere Street, which was a main route into Scotland. It also served as a supply depot when troops were on campaign further north.

When the forts along the Wall were built, this fort was not needed and its ramparts were taken down. Corbridge then developed into a garrison town, eventually covering 12 hectares. Its prosperity relied upon supplying the forts along the Wall, providing recreation for soldiers on leave and trading with local people.

By AD 180 substantial building projects were underway but some were never completed, owing perhaps to a serious threat from the north, which may also have necessitated the building of a wall around the two military compounds.

Many sculptures have been found proving that Corbridge, although on the edge of the empire, was quite an affluent town.

Granaries

These were built for long-term storage of food, especially grain which was the staple food of the soldiers. Their floors are raised off the ground to keep food dry and to reduce the risk of insect infestation. They also have ventilation slots along their sides to allow fresh air to circulate. To keep the buildings dry they had wide eaves which channelled rainwater well away from their sides and into stone drains that led into the main street drain. Both buildings had covered porticoes supported on columns, to keep water off the food as it was being unloaded. In front of the east granary is the stepped platform of the loading bay and there is a small entrance to the under-floor space in the front of the west granary. The buttresses down the sides of the granaries are close together, implying that they supported tall walls and a heavy stone roof. The row of pillars down the middle of the east granary suggests that it might have been two floors high. The two end columns of the east

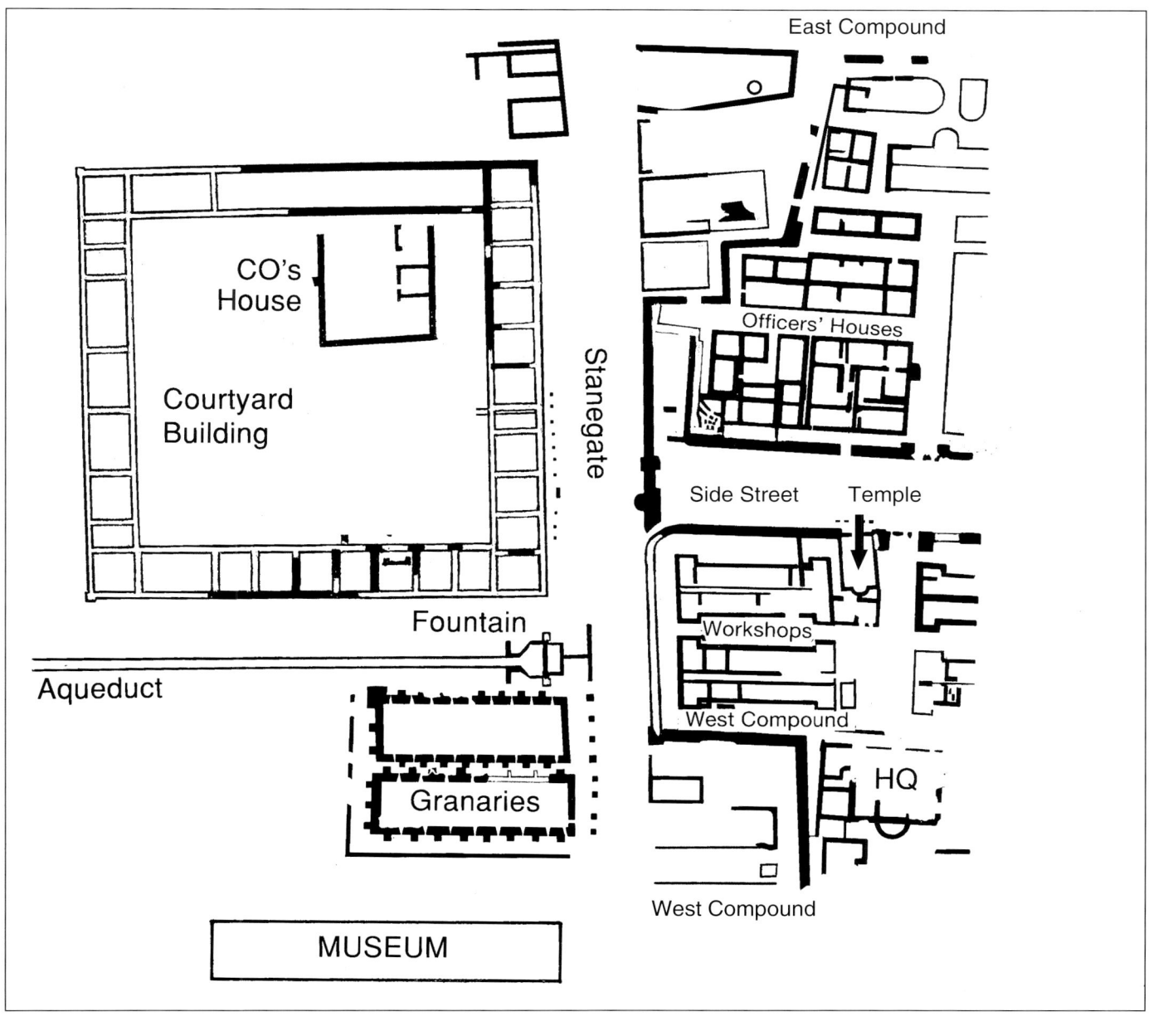

The granaries. Foodstuffs were stored on a raised floor around which air circulated to keep the food dry and to prevent damp.

granary are also wider than the rest and are constructed of courses of segmented stones, perhaps because they supported a greater weight.

The north east corner of the east granary has additional strengthening, again because it may have been a taller building.

Since the granaries were built, the level of the street has been raised through repeated resurfacing, and stone steps were added to carry supplies down to the level of the door into the granaries. Large stone slabs also needed to be placed between the columns to stop the road from falling into the spaces.

Fountain house and aqueduct
The town was supplied with water by an aqueduct. This consisted of an enclosed channel on top of an embankment. The base of the embankment remains, and a section of its stone channel has been rebuilt near the hedge. Either side of the embankment were stone drains that collected surface water which ran down its sides.

The aqueduct deposited water into a lead tank inside the fountain house. There it mixed with air to restore its freshness before flowing through spouts into the stone trough in front, from where people could collect water. The base of the trough has a hole to let water flow into a channel in the main street. This channel joins others and then flows under the street into two tanks in the side street.

The fountain house stands on a polygonal platform and was decorated with sculptures. Part of its ornamental pediment is in the museum. Either side of the building are stone blocks on which statues once stood. A long, wide groove shows where an ornamental screen was fitted. Slots in the upper surfaces of the stone blocks are for the iron clamps which held the blocks together.

Courtyard building
This large building, with four ranges around a courtyard, was never completed. Its intended use has not been established, but the fact that it has a moulded plinth and was to be constructed of large blocks of stone implies that it was to be quite an impressive building. Within its open space are the remains of an earlier stone fort. The fact that these remains had not been cleared is further evidence that the courtyard building was never completed.

The range that ran along the street was probably the only one that was built. It was divided into many smaller units and there are the bases of pillars for a portico along its length.

In the middle of the west range are sections of walls and a pile of

Providing pupils with a copy of this illustration will assist them in interpreting the remaining evidence and understanding the different components of the fountain house (see opposite).

Exposed foundations of the courtyard building.

stone blocks. The holes in their upper surfaces are Lewis holes, which were cut to assist lifting (see Resource Sheet 3). Other blocks have bumps on their sides, which were deliberately left on by the stonecutters at the quarry, again to assist lifting (see Resource Sheet 3). Once in place they would have been hacked off to create a flat surface. Many blocks are tapered in the middle; this is so that a pole can be inserted to manouevre them into position. A section of the foundations of this building has been exposed to show its construction.
In the middle of the south range is the entrance to the building, below which a large stone drain can be seen.

East compound

The walls of this compound do not enclose all the buildings, perhaps because they were not deemed important enough to be included. The function of most buildings in this compound is unclear, but two similar buildings arranged around a central courtyard are believed to be the homes of high ranking officers. These houses were later amalgamated into one when a hypocaust was installed in the north east room.

The other remains may have been those of a small headquarters building, a latrine and a barrack block.

West compound

The west compound contains a temple, which had been built before the compound was enclosed. The temple has a semi-circular recess at its west end which housed a statue, and the bases of four pillars were from from a small porch at its east end. The series of identically-shaped long back-to-back buildings may once have been barracks. They were later used as workshops as some rooms contain hearths and tanks, and iron spearheads and arrowheads were found in one room.

There are also the remains of a headquarters building with a small underground chamber. This may have been a strongroom which was usually found beneath the regimental shrine.

The fountain house. From here water was channelled to many parts of the site. The drains that are visible now would have been covered with stone slabs.

South Shields (Arbeia)

Situated beyond the easternmost point of Hadrian's Wall, on high ground on the south side of the River Tyne, this fort was probably built to guard the mouth of the river which was a main supply route for the troops manning the Wall. The present remains are probably those of the auxiliary fort built around AD 163 for 600 men. It replaced an earlier fort constructed by Hadrian, and was occupied for almost 300 years.

In AD 208 the size of the fort was increased to accommodate a total of 24 granaries, used for storing food to supply the campaigns of the Emperor Septimius Severus in Scotland. After Severus' campaigns ended, the fort may have been used as a permanent supply depot for part, if not all of Hadrian's Wall.

In the late third or early fourth century, fire destroyed many buildings, and these were replaced by twelve barracks. The garrison also changed when the fifth cohort of Gauls was replaced by a unit of bargemen from the River Tigris.

Remains of the fort's defences include stretches of fort wall and two gateways with corner towers. Inside there are the remains of two headquarters buildings (from different building periods). In the later building there is a strong room and offices with hypocausts. Nearby is a well from the earlier headquarters building. Other excavated buildings include parts of eight granaries, barracks, and a latrine block against the fort wall.

Full-size reconstructions have been made of the fort's west gate, a barrack block and part of the Commanding Officer's house, over the original foundations.

Wallsend Fort and the reconstructed bathhouse seen from the viewing tower.

South Shields Fort (Arbeia). The reconstructed west gate.

Wallsend (Segedunum)

This is the most eastern fort of the Wall and the most fully excavated, with the ground plan of virtually all its buildings marked out in gravel. It too was built to a standard Roman military plan. To the north end of the fort were six infantry barracks (partly hidden by a modern road). In the central section were the commanding officer's house, the headquarters building, double granary, hospital and water tank. The southern section contained cavalry barracks, and their recent discovery confirms that in the second century, cavalry soldiers lived in the rear room and stabled their horses in the front room. However, by the fourth century these barracks had been divided up into separate units, and the foundations of some of the dividing walls are still visible. In the corner of the site a bathhouse has been reconstructed, using the same plan as the one at Chesters.

Hadrian's Wall joins the west side of the fort as part of the southern tower of the west gate. Across the road is an 80 metre stretch of the Wall, including a collapsed section which is known to have been

Birdoswald Fort. The remains of the granaries.

Birdoswald

The fort at Birdoswald was built in a spectacular position above the Irthing Valley, and probably replaced an earlier turf and timber fort. Attached is a section of the Wall which was also originally built of turf, but was later rebuilt in stone. The section to the east is the longest continuous stretch of wall visible today and it has a number of inscriptions and markings along it. This leads to the milecastle at Harrow's Scar.

Most of the fort wall is visible, including three of its main gateways. The east gateway is one of the best preserved along the Wall; its two entrances and two towers stand to a good height. A tower at the north west corner of the fort wall contains the remains of two ovens. Within the fort are the remains of two granaries; their surviving features include buttresses, flagstone floors and ventilation systems. Nearby are the remains of a drill hall and workshops.

Earthworks inside the fort define the buried remains of the headquarters building, which is known to stand to a height of two metres. The line of the vallum and the original Turf Wall, which adjoined the east and west gateways, can also still be traced.

After the withdrawal of the Romans the site continued to be occupied. First, in the fifth century a timber hall was built, possibly for the use of a local chieftain. Later, a medieval tower house was constructed on the site, which was then replaced in the sixteenth century by a bastle house (fortified farmhouse) to protect the inhabitants from raids by the notorious 'Border reiver' families. Then in the seventeenth century a farmhouse was built, which has been extended on two other occasions.

Vindolanda

The first fort was built in the AD 80s on the Stanegate. Successive forts were built throughout the Roman occupation and the site was occupied for many years after AD 400.

The visible fort remains are largely fourth-century repairs of a fort built around AD 220. Two of the main buildings are currently visible: the headquarters building and the commanding officer's house. Inserted in the courtyard of the commanding officer's house is a later structure, almost certainly a Christian church of the early fifth century, the earliest such remains to be seen in Britain. South of the fort walls lies the early military bathhouse built around AD 100.

Outside the fort was an extensive civilian settlement. Visible remains are mainly family houses with shops and workshops attached. A military annexe from the Severan period lies within this area. The garrison was presumably guarding the inmates of a unique series of stone-built circular huts which then occupied the fort area. Also within the vicus is a temple and the later of Vindolanda's two excavated military bathhouses.

Beneath the visible remains are those of the earlier wooden forts. Although their wooden structures were not able to be preserved, many dramatic discoveries have been made including leather shoes, tents, textiles, wooden objects and, most famously, the Vindolanda writing tablets.

On site are reconstructions of a length of stone Wall with a turret, and a section of turf Wall with a timber milecastle gateway. Near to the museum are reconstructions of a Roman shop, house and temple.

Vindolanda Fort. Excavations have also revealed a substantial civilian settlement outside.

RESOURCE SHEET 1

Where did the Romans come from?

The soldiers who built the Wall did not come from Rome. Some came from the provinces where the legion was raised. Others were recruited from the provinces where the legion was posted. Consequently each legion could have consisted of men from many countries. The presence of thousands of soldiers building the Wall across the north of England would have brought people together from across the Roman Empire. Later units, sent to serve on the Wall from other parts of the Empire would have added to the rich cultural mix of people living along the frontier.

Building inscriptions, altars and tombstones tell us where they came from.

Fort	Origins of Units
South Shields	Iran
	Iraq
	France
Wallsend	Belgium
	Eastern France
	Upper Rhineland (Germany)
	Belgium
Newcastle	Welsh border
	Southern Bulgaria
	Turkey
Benwell	North-west Spain
	Upper Rhineland
Corbridge	Northern Spain
	France
Chesters	North-west Spain
	Upper Rhineland
	Yugoslavia
Carrawburgh	Belgium
	South-west France
	North Germany
	Holland
Housesteads	Belgium
	Germany
	Holland
Vindolanda	France
	Belgium
Great Chesters	Belgium
	Swiss/German
	Austrian border
	North-west Spain
Carvoran	Syria
	Croatia
Birdoswald	Belgium
	Dacia (Romania)
	Southern Bulgaria
	Turkey
Stanwix	France
Burgh by Sands	Germany
	Morocco
	Holland
Maryport	Spain
	Croatia
	Holland

D(is) M(anibus) Anicio Ingenuo medico ord(inario) coh(ortis) I Tungr(orum) uix(it) an(nos) XXV *'To the spirits of the departed and to Ancius Ingenuus, Surgeon of the 1st Cohort of Tungrians. He lived 25 years.'*

D(is) M(anibus) s(acrum) Dagvalda mil(es) Pan(noniorum) uixit an(nos) Pusinna (conniu)x titulu(m) pos(uit) *'To the spirits of the departed: Dagvalda, soldier of the Pannonians lived (?) years; his wife Pusinna set up this tombstone'.* (Chesters)

Using this information

Before or after your visit to Hadrian's Wall ask pupils to work in groups to locate the origins of the soldiers who built or served on the Wall. On a photocopied map they could draw lines to link the garrisons of each fort to their country of origin or they could use coloured threads on a large wall map.

Look at the extent of the Empire, suggesting possible reasons for its boundaries. Discuss how all these different nationalities communicated, using Latin as a common language, as seen on inscriptions.

As an extension activity you could ask pupils to work out how a soldier might have travelled to get to his fort on the Wall and how long it might have taken him.

RESOURCE SHEET 2

Building the Wall

This drawing has been adapted from a carving on Trajan's Column, which was erected in Rome in AD 113 to commemorate his campaigns in Dacia (Romania). It shows legionaries cutting logs and turf to construct a rampart. In the foreground soldiers are digging two ditches, while others are removing the earth in baskets or carrying turves on their shoulders. Some of the turves are held in place by short lengths of rope. The legionaries still wear their armour and carry their swords, but their javelins, helmets and shields are nearby (at the right of the drawing).

Using these images

Use these images to help pupils understand how the Wall was constructed and the enormity of this building project.

Begin by showing pupils both images and asking them to look for differences and similarities (larger copies are contained in the Hadrian's Wall poster pack). When pupils notice that the legionaries are wearing armour in only one of the images, ask them to suggest why. (It is probable that in the top image the legionaries are building a marching camp in hostile territory whereas in the bottom image the soldiers are building the Wall in an area, which has already been subdued.)

Then ask pupils to list:

- what materials are being used

- where the materials might have come from

- what tools are being used

- what jobs are being done.

Finally ask pupils to suggest all the different skills that were needed to carry out this huge building task.

This is an artist's impression showing how legionary soldiers might have constructed a stretch of Hadrian's Wall. It is based on research and archaeological evidence, and shows men carrying out a variety of building tasks. In the foreground a centurion is supervising his men; in the middle ground a commander is surveying the work and in the distance is one of the stone turrets, which were built prior to the Wall. In this image the legionaries are not wearing armour.

RESOURCE SHEET 3

Building the forts

Roman legions contained skilled builders, many of whom were masons who could carve stone for many different uses. The evidence of their work can be seen at each fort and settlement along the Wall, and identifying this will help pupils understand aspects of Roman building technology. The diagrams below will support teaching activities described later in the book.

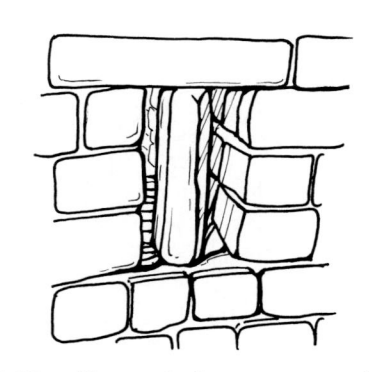

Corbridge

Foundations. To provide a sound base for the new forum building. Cobbles and older masonry were used.

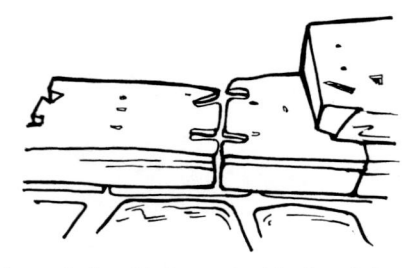

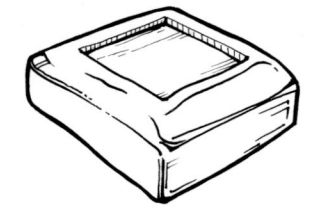

Square column base. To hold square columns for supporting a roof.

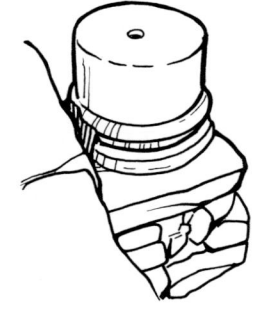

Columns. To support the roof of the granaries. The holes in their centre were for rods to keep each block in position.

Flues for box tiles. To carry warm air from under the floor up through the walls to heat a room in the HQ building of the earlier fort.

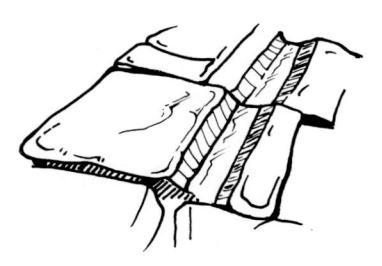

Mullion. To attach shutters to vents in the granaries in order to control flow of air.

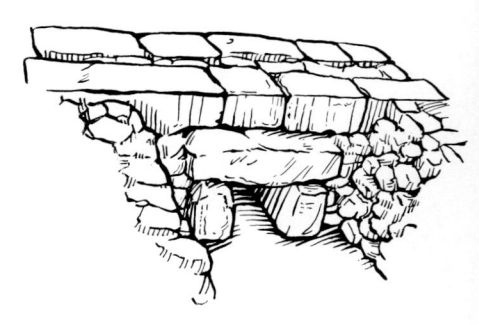

Clamp holes. To keep the blocks of the fountain house together.

Aqueduct channel. To supply the town with water.

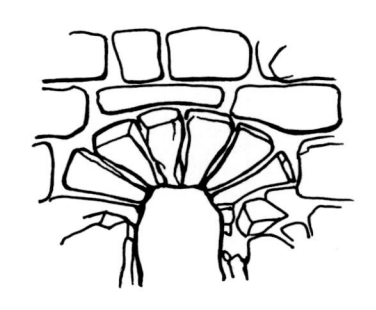

Guttering. To dispose of rainwater from the main road.

Drain. To carry waste underneath the courtyard building.

Tank. To collect water in the side street.

Culvert. To support the roof of a drainage channel in the west compound.

Tank. To collect roof water. The sides were grooved so that stone slabs could slot into each other.

Chesters bathhouse

These drawings highlight evidence that explains the design and function of the building.

Arched recesses in changing room.

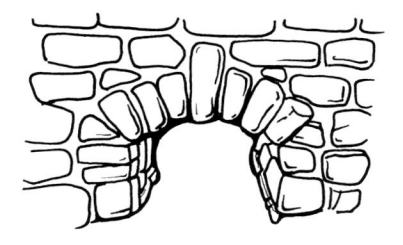

Stoke hole below hot dry room.

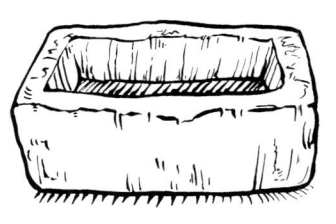

Trough in changing room.

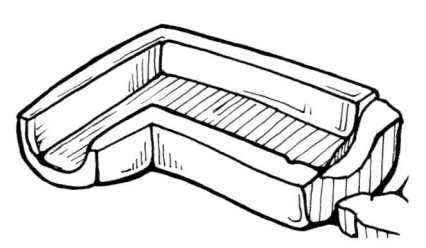

Stone channels to direct the flow of water.

Latrine drain.

Stone channel behind cold bath.

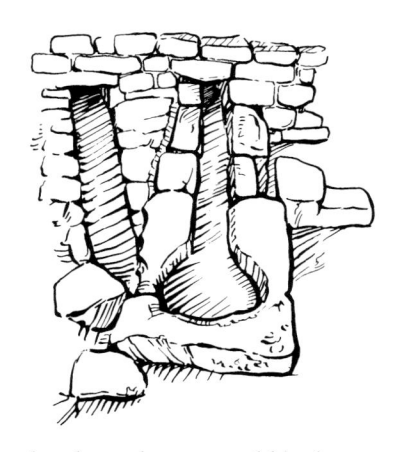

Circular channel next to cold bath.

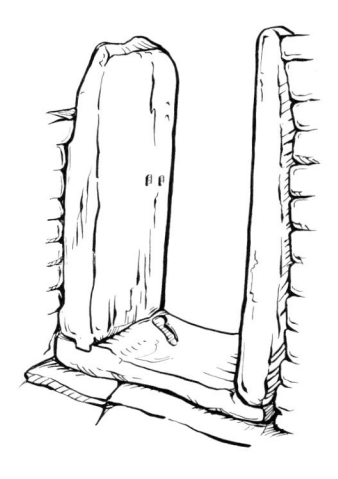

Door surround and slot for door post in hot dry room.

Diagrams of different lifting devices

Grips

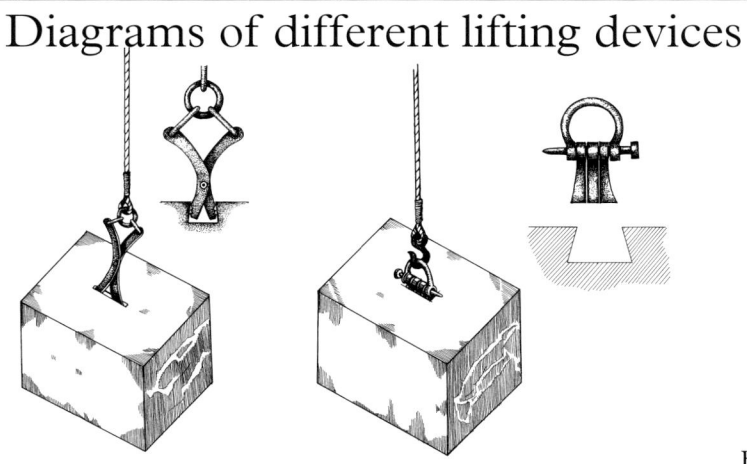

Interior grips

Lewis holes - cut into the top of the stone for inserting the grips.

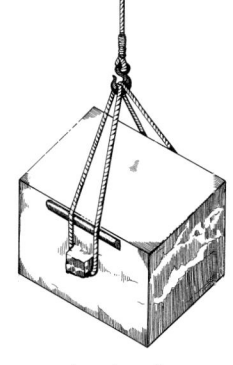

Bosses - chunks of stone were left on the sides to allow ropes to be attached. These would be hacked off when the stone was in place.

RESOURCE SHEET 4

Conquest and departure

The following text has been adapted from an account of the Battle of Mons Graupius in northern Scotland in AD 84. The original text was written by Tacitus, the son-in-law of Agricola, who led the campaign to conquer the north of Britain. It is written from the point of view of a foot soldier, and explains how a legion operates, and the tactics used by each side at the battle.

Ideas for using the text

■ Underline key words in the text and, after pupils have found their meaning in a dictionary, read the account again. Highlight words which are objective (factual) in one colour and those which are subjective (opinion) in another colour. Which side do they sympathise with and why?

■ Use one colour to underline words that refer to the numbers, weapons and tactics of the Roman army and another colour for the numbers, weapons and tactics of the Britons. A third colour could be used for the setting of the battle, highlighting the landscape and any built features.
  Alternatively, explain the differences between the two sides by collecting words and phrases to show what each side did, and listing them under two headings. Discuss how their tactics differed, and why so many Britons were defeated by so few Roman soldiers.

■ Ask pupils to imagine that they are one of the Britons who survived the battle. Tell their version of the story. Begin with, 'Today we were overcome by a callous and cold-blooded army.' End the story with, 'The enemy lost three hundred and sixty men. We lost ten thousand brave warriors'.

Battle of Mons Graupius

As the sun rose, Agricola positioned eight thousand of us infantrymen alongside three thousand cavalry. We stood strong in the centre, with the cavalry on our wings. The legionaries were positioned in front of the palisade, as a show of pride should we gain victory without the loss of Roman blood. It was a fearful sight looking at the thousands of Britons spread on the distant hills. They seemed to tower high above us. On the flat plain between them and us their war chariots jostled noisily for space. We were greatly outnumbered. In fact there were so many Britons that Agricola feared they would attack our front and sides at the same time. So he ordered us to spread out. As we waited nervously Agricola got down from his horse and stood in front of us, confident of victory. I no longer felt afraid.

The battle began suddenly, and at first both sides fought at long range. The Britons, with their long swords and small shields, brushed aside our missiles with great skill and retaliated with dense volleys of spears. Agricola then ordered us forward. The long swords of the Britons were not suited to hand to hand fighting. Our swords are short and sharp and we stabbed at faces and struck hard with the bosses of our shields and began to push up the hill. Other battalions of our army followed and slaughtered anyone near. We moved with such speed that we sometimes left the enemy behind, slightly wounded or even unharmed.

Meanwhile, the cavalry had routed the enemy's chariots. Their first charge had not been easy, as the solid ranks of the enemy and the rough ground brought our cavalry to a standstill. For a moment some began to panic, but we held firm.

Thousands of Britons stood on the hilltops watching the battle below. They laughed at our small numbers and slowly began to descend, surrounding our army. But Agricola expected this and ordered four squadrons of cavalry that he had kept back for emergencies, to charge at them furiously. They scattered and we began a glorious pursuit, taking prisoners, but then killing them as new enemies appeared. The Britons were felled in huge numbers but showed great courage even in defeat. Small groups even gathered together and charged at us unarmed, sacrificing themselves to their gods. Weapons, corpses, limbs and blood covered the ground.

Despite their huge losses the Britons still did not give up. Some grouped together in the woods to ambush our men as we followed them in. Agricola was everywhere at once, and he ordered us to discard our large shields and form a ring around the woods. Then he sent the cavalry in for the kill, and where the trees were dense, they dismounted and hunted on foot. The Britons were no match for the ordered ranks of our soldiers. They disbanded again and ran for their lives. By nightfall it was all over. The enemy lost ten thousand men this day, but we only lost three hundred and sixty.

The Roman Centurion's Song
Rudyard Kipling

Legate, I had the news last night - my cohort ordered home
By ships to Portus Itius and thence by road to Rome.
I've marched the companies aboard, the arms are stowed below:
Now let another take my sword. Command me not to go!

I've served in Britain forty years, from Vectis to the Wall,
I have none other home than this, nor any life at all.
Last night I did not understand, but now the hour draws near
That calls me to my native land, I feel that land is here.

Here where men say my name was made, here where my work was done;
Here where my dearest dead are laid, my wife, my wife and son;
Here where time, custom, grief and toil, age, memory, service, love,
Have rooted me in British soil. Ah, how can I remove?

For me this land, that sea, these airs, those folk and fields suffice
What purple southern pomp can match our changeful northern skies,
Black with December snows unshed or pearled with August haze
The clanging arch of steel-grey March, or June's long-lighted days?

You'll follow widening Rhodanus till vine and olive lean
Aslant before the sunny breeze that sweeps Nemausus clean
To Arelate's triple gate; but let me linger on,
Here where our stiff-necked British oaks confront Euroclydon!

You'll take the old Aurelian Road through shore-descending pines
Where, blue as any peacock's neck, the Tyrrhene Ocean shines.
You'll go where laurel crowns are won, but will you e'er forget
The scent of hawthorn in the sun, or bracken in the wet?

Let me work here for Britain's sake, at any task you will
A marsh to drain, a road to make or native troops to drill.
Some western camp (I know the Pict) or granite Border keep,
Mid seas of heather derelict, where our old messmates sleep.

Legate, I come to you in tears. My cohort ordered home!
We served in Britain forty years. What should I do in Rome?
Here is my heart, my soul, my mind, the only life I know.
I cannot leave it all behind. Command me not to go!

Ideas for using the poem

- Compare the descriptions of Britain to that of the Mediterranean region. Discuss the meaning of phrases such as: *'Purple southern pomp'* (purple is the colour worn by the emperor and his family); *'Where laurel crowns are won'* (a crown of laurel was given to victors of battles and contests); *'Mid seas of heather derelict, where our old messmates sleep'*.

- Ask pupils to give three reasons why the centurion wanted to stay in Britain. Then, imagining that he is their husband or father, write a letter to the Legate pleading for him to be allowed to stay.

- Write a similar poem based around a soldier who is looking forward to leaving Britain and returning to Italy. Or, based on site work and pupils' impressions of a visit to the Wall, ask them to imagine themselves to be the ghost of a Roman soldier who has returned to his military posting eighteen hundred years later. What would be his thoughts?

- Use descriptions in the poem to paint a picture of Italy based on the phrase such ad: *'Through shore descending pines where blue as any peacock's neck, the Tyrrene Ocean shines'*, or of Britain based on the phrase: *'Changeful northern skies. Black with December snows unshed'*. If you do this after your visit to a site, you can combine pupils' own impressions.

Place names

Portus Itius - Boulogne
Nemausus - Nîmes
Aurelian Road - main road from Rome up the west coast of Italy
Tyrrhene Sea - sea off the west coast of Italy
Legate - Governor or commanding officer of a legion
Vectis - Isle of Wight
Arelate - Arles
Rhodanus - River Rhône
Euroclydon - strong, south-east wind

Educational approaches

Planning your visit

If your visit to Hadrian's Wall is in support of a study of Roman Britain there is a scheme of work on the following pages to help you integrate this into your teaching. You could use it as an alternative to the three sections in the current QCA scheme - A Roman Case Study - that looks at Boudicca and the rebellion of AD 60.

When choosing which site to visit, bear in mind that you will not be able to give pupils an overview of every aspect of life in Britain under Roman occupation. Each site offers different opportunities and you should choose the site that best suits your teaching objectives.

Use your preparatory visit to select areas where you want pupils to work. Suggestions of places to work at each site and activities to do there are given in the following pages. These activities will also encourage the development of pupils' skills in historical enquiry and stimulate their thinking. However, they represent only one approach, and you may choose to develop your own ideas for investigating the site.

Using helpers

Consider placing your helpers at focus areas, rather than asking them to remain with one group throughout the visit. By supervising only one activity they will soon gain confidence in their own knowledge of that particular area and the skills you want pupils to practise. Give helpers copies of the site plan and the educational activities you want them to lead. (Laminated copies of the suggested activities for each site are available from the custodian). To facilitate control of your class use a whistle to signal when individual groups should move onto another area or to assemble the whole group (whistles can also be loaned from the custodians).

Understanding the sites

It is not essential that you know everything about the site you are going to visit. Even archaeologists are not sure. Do not worry if you cannot answer pupils' questions. Work with them to use the surviving evidence to suggest possible answers. Even if they turn out not to be accurate, you are giving them an opportunity to practise using different historical enquiry skills. Allow time for pupils to make their own discoveries, even if they are to be escorted around the site in groups. Invite comment on the site and its situation within the wider landscape.

On arrival

Make sure pupils and helpers know where the toilets are. Agree a time and location for lunch and for meeting up at the end of the visit. Decide with the custodian how you will organise visits to the shop.

First impressions

All sites consist of low walls and open grassed areas where the site has not been excavated. Also, there may be only a few other visitors on the day of your visit. None of these will give an impression of the enclosed, and perhaps cramped, conditions in which hundreds of men lived and worked. You should therefore impress upon pupils that this would not have been the scene when the fort was occupied. A good discussion point at the beginning of your visit to Chesters or Housesteads is to ask pupils what they expected to see at the fort. Identify what is missing and discuss why.

Familiarisation activities

These are useful activities to set on arrival as they provide a purposeful means for pupils to explore the site and to expend some energy if they have been sitting on the coach for some time. They can also be used to develop pupils' observation and deductive skills, the results of which can be used for follow-up work back at school. Meanwhile you can use the time to explain what you want your helpers to do and let them familiarise themselves with any tasks or areas you want them to supervise. The suggested activities for each site begin with a familiarisation task.

Information panels

All sites have information panels, often with artist's impressions which help you to explain how each building was used. When looking at them you should explain to pupils that they only show how the buildings might have looked like, and that people's interpretations of the remains can differ.

Artists' impressions are very useful for developing pupils' historical thinking, particularly those of enquiry and of interpreting evidence. On site, stand by a panel and ask pupils to match the surviving parts of the building in front of them with the artist's impression. Then look for clues that might have helped the artist show the missing parts. Finally discuss ways that the artist might have been able to work out what the rest of the building looked like.

Recording information

Avoid spending too much time writing down information, especially if the weather is poor. Observations can be recorded using only key words or quick annotated sketches. Groups of pupils could also use a disposable camera, though you should ensure that they note down the subject of each picture on a plan of the site after each photograph has been taken.

Museums

Free teacher booklets are available to help you use the exceptional collections in the museums at Corbridge and Chesters. The museum at Housesteads is smaller and, as such can only be used by small groups. Thre is also a large handling collection at Corbridge with teacher's notes.

Adverse weather

The museums can be a useful retreat in bad weather provided pupils are working on directed tasks, and you are advised to keep some activities in reserve. Alternatively, you could take with you the ground plans of individual buildings (photocopied from the plans earlier in this book), and in the museum ask pupils to find, and either draw or list the objects that would have been used inside one or more buildings. Or, as a group activity, ask pupils to find four objects that might have been used in each of the main buildings on the site.

At Housesteads you could ask the custodian whether the school's base is free if you have not already booked it.

Walking by the Wall

If you are also going to walk alongside stretches of Hadrian's Wall you could take with you laminated copies of some of the images in this book. They can be used to explain surviving structures as you come across them, and to explain how the Wall was constructed.

Observations or impressions recorded on site could be translated into artwork back at school.

LEARNING OBJECTIVES	TEACHING ACTIVITIES	LEARNING OUTCOMES	POINTS TO NOTE AND CURRICULUM LINKS
CHILDREN SHOULD LEARN	**Why was Hadrian's Wall built?**	CHILDREN	
why the Romans wanted to conquer Britain	Ask children why the Romans might want to bring Britain under their control, eg *corn, silver, wool, slaves*. Use maps of the Empire to show distances and boundaries.	explain the Romans' interest in controlling Britain	
how the Roman army was able to defeat a much larger Scottish force	Compare and contrast the fighting methods of the Romans and native British. Explain the differences in armour and weaponry by making labelled drawings (see curriculum links for other, practical activities). Discuss how the Roman army under Agricola defeated the native tribes at the Battle of Mons Graupius in Scotland in AD 84. Use Tacitus' account of Agricola's campaigns ***. Extracts could be adapted for use in the literacy hour. Children could write an article about the battle as if they were reporters at the scene, or pretend to be a veteran soldier recounting it to his grandson.	explain how the Roman army was successful in conquest	Use sources to explain Roman weaponry and tactics. Examine the design of Roman armour by making replica sections using available materials. Links with PE: Practise marching drills and formation work outside (movement and coordination). Links with Maths: Calculate how long it would take to march from one fort to the nearest turret milecastle or fort, with full marching kit or in response to an anticipated attack.
the reasons why the Romans withdrew from Scotland	Discuss why the Roman army was unable to overpower Scotland and why it eventually withdrew. (The native people held onto their territory because they knew the land and could use guerrilla tactics to attack. Also, some troops were withdrawn to deal with rebellions in other parts of the Empire.)	suggest reasons why the occupying forces were unable to conquer Scotland	Links with Art: Celtic face painting (or masks); designs on Roman and Celtic shields and standards.
that Hadrian ordered the construction of a Wall across the north of England	Discuss reasons why Hadrian chose this part of England as his frontier, why he decided upon a wall as his means of control and what functions he expected it to fulfil. Children could then compose an Imperial proclamation, outlining his intentions and instructions. If time permits, they could compare his reasons from the viewpoint of the local natives and the soldiers who were to build it. All the events of this section could be presented as a storyboard or as a cartoon sequence.	suggest reasons why Hadrian built the Wall and what purpose he intended it to fulfil	You may want to mention that the next emperor, Antoninus Pius, abandoned the Wall and resumed attempts to conquer Scotland. These failed and the Wall was reinstated as the frontier. Point out that no records survive and that historians are not sure of Hadrian's motives.
how Hadrian's Wall might have been built	**What was Hadrian's Wall?** Explain that building the Wall was a major task that required the mobilisation and maintenance of thousands of soldiers, as well as the acquisition and transport of substantial amounts of different materials. Use artists' impressions of the Wall under construction or carvings from Trajan's Column to list what materials, tools, jobs and skills were needed ***.	explain how the Roman army was able to undertake such a huge building project	Links with English: Ask pupils to imagine themselves as one of the figures in the picture. What might that person and others be saying or thinking, eg *issuing orders, explaining tasks, giving instructions, asking for help or giving encouragement*. Links with PE (movement): Simulate building tasks through working in pairs or as a team.
that the Wall was only one part of the frontier's defences	Show children a range of images of Hadrian's Wall frontier. Ask them to identify military features, eg *forts, turrets, milecastles, roads, bridges, vallum and ditches*, producing labelled drawings or annotated plans to explain their design and function ***. This activity could be undertaken before or after a visit to the frontier.	can identify and explain the different parts of the frontier zone use primary and secondary evidence to describe what the Wall might have looked like	Links with Geography: Children could use a map to find out how close they are to the line of the Wall. Do they live behind or beyond the frontier? Links with Science (materials): Point out that the western part of the Wall was initially constructed using turf.
that the Romans used a standard plan for their forts and the buildings in them	Give children plans of forts (from guidebooks) and ask them to identify similarities and differences. Which buildings are always contained inside and why? They could work in pairs to make a labelled plan of a typical fort; in groups to design a fort using paper templates to represent different buildings; or as a class to make a model using paper or card. Discuss the advantages of building forts to a standard design by imagining that	describe the shape, siting and layout of a typical Roman fort, and explain why this layout was used	Links with Technology: How the Romans used stone as a multi-purpose building material. Look for different examples on site, eg *hypocaust systems and the methods of supplying, storing and distributing water*. Find out what devices Roman builders used to lift stone.

Learning objectives	Teaching activities	Children should learn	Points to note / Links
to identify the surviving evidence of the Hadrian's Wall frontier	children are troops who have just arrived at their new posting or are responding to an alarm raised during the night. Visit Hadrian's Wall frontier. Decide on a focus for your visit. It could be: • what the Wall looked like, and its impact on the landscape • its different defences, and how they functioned • the different buildings in which soldiers lived and worked • artefacts in museums that show how soldiers and civilians lived.	present information that shows an understanding of Hadrian's Wall frontier	Links with Geography: Use aerial photographs to look at the siting of the Wall, its related structures and earthworks, and its impact on the landscape.
how this evidence enables us to formulate an impression of what the frontier looked like and what it might have been like to live alongside it	Use artists' impressions to help children understand the remains of a site. Talk about how people are able to 'reconstruct' buildings from the past and where the evidence comes from, eg *archaeological evidence, documentary and visual sources, and comparison with similar buildings*. Compare two versions of a similar subject. (See Interpreting the Past poster pack for images and further ideas.) After the visit encourage children to establish what they have learned, and what else they would like to find out. Let them frame their own questions for independent research.	understand how artists' impressions, models and reconstructed buildings can be produced from limited evidence, and how interpretations can differ	Links with English: Recollections and information recorded during a site visit can be used to inspire different forms of language work. Children could imagine what it might have been like on look-out duty at a turret or milecastle, on guard duty at a fort, or a visitor to a town or civilian settlement. What would they see, hear and feel in each situation?
	What was the impact of Hadrian's Wall on life in the region?		
how the construction of the Wall affected the lives of the local population	Explain that the line of the Wall followed strategic land features, often cutting through tribal homelands. Discuss with children what life would be like if an invading force built a wall through the middle of their town or village.	appreciate that the Wall cut through tribal homelands and divided its people	Opportunities for role-play. Create a barrier across the classroom with a controlled crossing point, challenging pupils each time they want to pass.
how the frontier brought peace to the area and encouraged migration to the region	Explain how the frontier included a network of roads. This allowed troops to move quickly in response to trouble and gave stability to the region. This encouraged further settlement and trade. On a map of the area in Roman times ask children to work out routes between forts, towns and ports.	explain how the frontier brought peace and stability to the area	Links with Technology: Look at possible ways that soldiers could relay messages along the Wall.
	Supplying the troops created a military-based economy which benefited local people and also brought merchants from throughout the Empire. Divide children into groups, asking each to list what different people might need, eg *officer in charge of the fort's stores, commanding officer, soldier, tribal leader or civilian*. In two adjacent columns say where each item might have come from and how it was transported.	explain how the construction of the Wall encouraged migration to the area and introduced new settlement	Use handling collections to look at what objects were used for, where they came from and how they were transported.
how different people viewed the construction of the Wall	Ask children what the Wall might have meant to Hadrian, the soldiers building the Wall, and the native people living either side of it. Summarise their views on a chart under three columns, or attach speech bubbles around three large character drawings.	recognise that the Wall had a different meaning for various groups of people	Point out that the native population did not become Romans, but that some adopted Roman lifestyles while many others retained their old lifestyle.
about the origins of the soldiers who served on the Wall, many of whom retained their own traditions and beliefs	Give children a map of the Roman Empire or modern western world. Ask them to find where soldiers at each fort came from ***. Draw a line connecting the country to the relevant forts. Children could imagine how a soldier building the Wall might feel when looking at a map that showed his homeland. What might he say to his family about north Britain, his comrades and the local people? Compare his feelings with those of the centurion in the Kipling poem *'A Centurion's Song'*, who has been recalled from Britain after a long period of service ***.	give reasons for the multi-cultural nature of people living in the Wall area	Links to Citizenship: Discuss origins of children's families, friends and neighbours. Point out that the Romans had a multicultural society in which the common language was Latin. This enabled all races to communicate, and was essential in the army so that soldiers could follow orders and work as a team.

*** **Resource is contained in this handbook.**

Housesteads Fort

Housesteads Fort is on a steep, exposed slope with a sheer drop on the north side. Independent investigation is not advisable for pupils at KS2 or below. Instead you are recommended to divide your class into smaller groups to work under the supervision of helpers. Groups could follow a prescribed route around the fort, setting off at intervals, or they could begin at different parts of the site. Give helpers copies of these pages, highlighting those activities or discussion points you want them to lead. If the site is busy it might be advisable to set a time limit for your activities at each area.

Familiarisation activity

Plan an introductory trail around the site for small groups led by helpers. Stick a plan of the fort in the middle of a sheet with six boxes around the edge. Mark out a route, stopping at six places, and in the boxes collect words or short phrases to describe what is there. Suggested places are the latrines, the headquarters building, the hospital, the granaries, the barracks and the north gate, where there is an excellent vantage point of the Wall.

Hospital

Use this building to encourage pupils to make their own deductions about how each of the rooms might have been used.
Help them decide by beginning with the following questions: why would the largest room be next to the main entrance? why are there so many other smaller rooms? how might the courtyard have been used?
You could follow this by giving pupils a photocopy of the artist's impression of the building on page 12 and ask them to compare it with the artist's impression on the information panel. Look for differences, especially the columns, roof, windows and tiles, and ask pupils to give reasons why the two images are different.

North gate

Use this location to impress upon pupils the impact of the Wall on the area and the consequence of a solid barrier across the north of England. Observe the route of the Wall eastwards. How was its course influenced by the landscape? How might a guard on duty hre feel when looking north or east? Stand quietly facing out and ask pupils to list words to describe what they can see, hear and feel. Share feelings and use pupils' responses for creative writing back at school.

Granaries

Use the granaries to help pupils work out how we can tell from limited evidence how a building functioned.

■ Begin by identifying the different parts of the buildings. (Columns to support raised floor, joist holes to hold floor timbers, side vents, loading bays, row of pillars down the centre and the buttresses against the walls.)

■ Explain that the granaries were used to store food securely and to keep it fresh and dry.

■ Ask what conditions are needed to store food in such a way. (Cool, dry environment, precautions against vermin, and security features to prevent theft.)

Headquarters building

The headquarters building has three distinct areas - the courtyard, cross-hall and offices - and can be used for a surveying and planning activity.
Give pupils an outline plan of the building (see page 11), marking the walls separating the three areas. Then ask pupils to locate and draw features that help show how parts of the building might have looked like or how it was used. The level of detail will obviously depend upon how much time you allow for the task and the ability of your pupils.

■ In the courtyard look for the main entrance and doorway into the cross-hall; the column bases and walls of the colonnade; the stone flagging and gutters; and the remains of hearths in the rooms around the sides.

■ In the cross-hall look for columns of the aisle; the raised platform used by the commanding officer; and the decorated base for inscriptions and statues. From here pupils can view the remains of the offices and the shrine, where they can look for the grooves for the stone screen which controlled access into it.
It was usual to have a strong room below the shrine. Discuss why this was not possible at Housesteads, and ask pupils to suggest which room would have been the best room to use instead.

■ Then ask pupils to suggest how the remains of the building show how this was done. (Food was kept fresh and cool by the flow of air through the vents. It was kept dry and free of vermin by being stored on a raised floor. The building itself was kept dry by having a very wide roof which channeled rainwater away from its sides - the extent of the buttresses show the width of the roof.
Food was delivered via the loading bays through doors which were secured - look for sockets for pivots, the doorstop and the sill.

■ Tell pupils that the granaries were once one single building. Can they look for evidence to show this?

Barracks

Use the barracks to make deductions about the living conditions of the troops and their centurion.

■ Before looking at the interpretation panels walk down the street between the barrack blocks. Ask pupils to describe the shape of the buildings and to suggest what they think they might be. Then look at the panel.

■ Return to the barracks and ask pupils to explain how we know that they were divided later into separate 'chalets'.

■ Find the centurion's house at the end and compare its size to a barrack room. Why did he have such a large space?

Discuss what living conditions might have been like for the hundreds of troops, living eight to a barrack. Today, the low walls allow you to see the surrounding countryside, but when built, the fort was surrounded by high walls with buildings close to each other.

Artist's impression of the commanding officer's house.

Commanding officer's house

This building was a substantial house with many clues to help pupils work out how various rooms were used. By comparing this building to their own homes, pupils can gain some impression of domestic life in a large Roman household.

In pairs ask pupils to find the following areas:
■ main entrance
■ paved courtyard
■ kitchen with a raised oven in the corner
■ latrines with drains leading from it
■ dining room with a heated floor
■ stables with trough and drains.

Take them to the dining room and look for evidence to show this, and probably other rooms, were heated. Direct them to the remains of a furnace and flue to the west of the room; the raised floor constructed of stacks and reused columns; and recesses in the walls which contained box tiles to carry warm air from the furnace up through the walls. You may need to explain their function to pupils.

Conclude by asking pupils what the lifestyle was like for the people who lived in this house, and how different it would have been to everyone else living in the fort.

East and west gates

Use the gates to give pupils an opportunity of working with limited evidence to explain how a building looked and functioned. Begin by asking them to describe three distinctive features of the design of a gateway. (Shape of features, size of masonry, number of passageways, gates and guardchambers.) Then ask pupils to describe three features to show how the gates operated. (Sockets for door posts, gate sills and the stop block for the doors.) Perhaps ask pupils to sketch the ground plan, and compare it to other gateways. Pupils could demonstrate their understanding by pretending to be guards on duty when a group of Britons are seen approaching (either hostile or friendly). What will the guards do? Where would they stand? How do they open and close the gates?

Another approach is to give them an artist's impression of one of the gateways, (see page 11) and ask them to identify the evidence that has enabled the artist to make his drawing.

Latrines

Use this building to investigate the ingenuity of Roman plumbing and building technology.

■ Ask pupils to trace the flow of water from the tanks to the latrines, then find the channels that supplied additional water. Which direction did the water flow and why?

■ Find the plugholes that controlled the flow of water from the tanks. (They were probably plugged by a rag-covered stick.)

■ Look at how the stone slabs of the tanks fitted together. Find the lead that sealed the joints and coated the iron clamps to prevent them from rusting.

■ Discuss why the sides of the tanks are worn. (Soldiers leaning over to wash clothing.)

Corbridge Town

The site is enclosed, and from any one position you will be able to supervise your group. You can therefore set activities that enable pupils to move around independently. There are many different types of buildings here, and the approaches below refer to the most easily understood buildings, and require pupils to be split into smaller groups.

Familiarisation activity

At Corbridge, stone has been used for a wide range of building purposes, and looking for different examples will be a useful familiarisation activity. Use the drawings on the resource sheet on page 24 to prepare a find-and-seek activity. Place them around the edge of a sheet with a plan of the site in the centre. Photocopy it and give copies to pairs of pupils, asking them to find each feature and then draw a line showing where the feature can be found on the plan.

Temple

Use this building for a matching activity where pupils have to look at the evidence to decide how the complete building might have looked.

Give pupils copies of artists' impressions of different temples (available from the custodian). Ask them to look at each one carefully, comparing it with the remaining evidence to decide what type of temple would most likely have been there. If time permits, take pupils to the museum and look for objects that might have been inside the temple. Discuss the function of these objects and where they might have been used in the temple - inside, outside, by the door, in the middle or inside the apse.

Officers' houses

These two houses are believed to be those of officers (ignore the later, outer walls when they were amalgamated into one house). Use them for an activity to develop pupils' surveying, planning and deducting skills.

Give pupils a plan showing only the basic square outline of the building and go to the northern house. Tell them to find and mark the main entrance and the small courtyard, then show how it was divided up into smaller rooms, marking their doorways. Finally sketch any features that could help them explain what each room might have been used for. Encourage them to work out how other rooms might have been used by asking them to imagine that they were an officer and this was their home. Which room would they have used to stable their horse, store their uniform and equipment, to bathe, to eat or to entertain friends? Which room might have been the kitchen or accommodation for his servant or slave? Record their decisions on the plan.

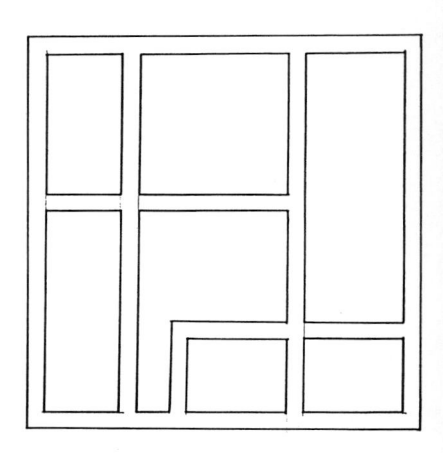

Plan of an officer's house.

Fountain house and water supply

Use these features to help pupils appreciate the ingenuity of Roman builders in supplying and distributing water throughout the town.

■ Start at the northern edge of the site at the reconstructed water channel near the hedge. Point out that this would have been on top of a nearby mound of earth. ■

■ Follow the course of the aqueduct to the fountain house.

■ At the fountain house ask pupils to describe how the slabs of the tank are held together, and to suggest why the edges of the tank are so worn.

■ Trace the route of the different channels that lead from the tank and see how far each one goes.

Give pupils photocopies of the line drawing of the fountain house on page 18. Stand in front of the building and ask pupils to colour those parts that are still there. Then ask them to suggest how the artist was able to show the parts that are no longer there. Let them look closely at the remains for clues.

As a role-play activity you could ask pupils to pretend to be a builder who has been asked to rebuild the fountain house. Give pupils copies of the line drawing or the artist's impression (copies can be loaned from the custodian) and ask them to describe what needs to be done.

The granaries

Use the two granaries to help pupils work out the function of a building from close observation of limited evidence.

■ Begin by asking pupils to compare the two buildings, making a list to show how they are similar and different.

■ Then, starting from the north end, follow the drains around the building. Help pupils to make simple deductions, such as where the water would have come from (the roof). Why were the drains built in this exact position? (To catch water dripping off the roof.) Why was it important to keep the water away from walls of the building? (To prevent damp.) Why were the buildings surrounded so closely by a wall? (For security.)

Develop pupils' skills further by asking the following questions.

■ What evidence is there to show that the building was constructed to keep food dry and fresh? (The raised floor; the vents at ground level; the surrounding drain to carry away water. This indicates the width of the roof which needed to be very wide to keep the sides of the building dry.)

■ What evidence is there to show that these buildings were constructed to store things? (The plain stonework; the lack of doors apart from those at the front; the thick floor slabs for supporting a heavy weight; the surrounding wall to prevent theft; and the large buttresses against the outside walls to counteract internal pressure.)

■ What evidence indicates that the east granary may have been taller or two floors high? (The row of columns down the centre; the thicker columns at the front that may have supported a greater weight, and the additional reinforcement at the north-east corner.)

Artist's impression of the buildings along the Stanegate.

Comparing the granaries

Similarities
Four columns at the front
Shape and size
Thickness of walls
Construction of walls
Thick slabs for floor
Buttresses
Vents at ground level
Surrounded by drains
Surrounded by a wall

Differences
Spacing between columns
Construction of columns
Small entrance to hypocaust in west granary
Loading bay on east granary
Central row of columns in east granary

Courtyard building

This extensive building was never completed, but you can use it to give an indication of the growth and size of the town, and to demonstrate many aspects of Roman building technology.

■ Begin by asking pupils to count how many shops or offices there are on the range that faces the Stanegate, then work out how many different premises there could there have been altogether in this building. What does this suggest about the size of Corbridge and its population and the occupation of many of its inhabitants?

■ Compare the quality of the stonework with the earlier fort buildings still visible in the courtyard. What does this say about the status of this building?

■ Go to the east range and use the 'Stonework resource' sheet to explain how large blocks of stone were lifted and positioned. Ask pupils to find evidence to show this. Look at the exposed foundations to show how buildings were constructed.

To communicate their findings you could ask pupils to decide on a series of photographs that explains each building stage and then write brief instructions for each image to describe what the builders did. They could show the preparation of the cobbled sub-surface, the laying of large foundation stones, the blocks being lifted and manoeuvred into position, and the final smoothing and plastering of the walls.

Chesters Fort

All the excavated remains are contained within fenced enclosures, and apart from the bath house near the river, the whole site is visible from one central point, making free movement and independent work possible.

Familiarisation activity
Analysing and comparing the gateways is an excllent familiarisation activity. First, ask pupils to walk around the perimeter of the site and count how many entrances there are into the fort. Then divide your class into four groups, sending each to a different gateway. Ask them to write down at least three features that might help them work out what the entrance looked like, then three features to show how the gates opened and closed. Or, you could ask pupils to make a basic sketch of the ground plan. Let pupils briefly visit other gateways to corroborate their findings. Bring the class together and compare their information. How are the gateways similar or different?

Barracks

Use the barrack blocks to make deductions about the living conditions of the troops and to make comparisons with those of their officer.

■ Walk down the road between the barracks to the officer's house at the end. Ask pupils to look for the entrances into each barrack, and to suggest what the columns in front might have been for, and why there were drains in the middle of the road. Point out that these were not the only barracks in the fort, there were many more, but only two blocks have been excavated.

■ Divide your group in half, one for each block, giving each the following two activities to do.

■ Measure a barrack room. Ask pupils how they would organise the space if this was their living space. (Each room housed eight soldiers who may have slept on wooden bunks.) Where would they have stored their equipment? As this was a cavalry fort where do pupils think the horses were kept?

■ Count how many rooms the officer had. Compare this with the space the soldiers had. Why might he have had larger living accommodation? Suggest how he might have used the different rooms.

Commanding officer's house

Use this large building which had a number of alterations and additions to look for clues that show change.

■ At the information panel explain the original layout and size of the house. Point out that other rooms were added later inside the central courtyard. As no-one knows why they were built you could ask pupils to think of possible reasons.

■ Ask pupils to work out how many rooms were added, and how many had hypocausts. Do this by entering the building by the entrance opposite the barrack block and identifying rooms by looking for their worn thresholds and the sockets for door posts. What can pupils deduce about the lifestyle of the people who lived in these rooms, and what they might have been used for?

■ Another addition was the private bath suite. How do we know it was added later? Look at the hypocausts and ask pupils to describe the different ways that the stacks were made. Is there any evidence of recycling? Look for the furnace and stoke hole that supplied hot air to the underfloor. What materials are used here and why? (Tile, unlike stone, would not crack when exposed to extreme heat.) Ask pupils why the commanding officer would have had his own bath house.

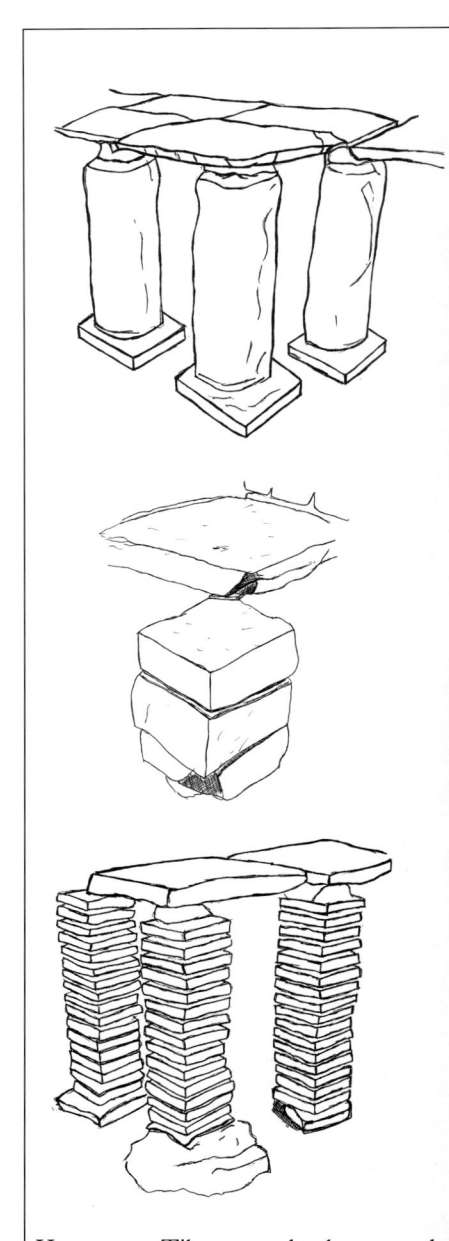

Hypocaust. Tiles, reused columns and blocks of stones were used to support the floor which enabled warm air from furnaces to circulate and heat floors in the commanding officer's house.

Bathhouse

Use this exceptional building to investigate the ingenuity of Roman plumbing.

For an introductory task you could use the drawings on the resource sheet on page 25 to prepare a find-and-seek activity. Place these drawings on a sheet of paper with a plan of the bathhouse in the middle. Give photocopies to pairs of pupils, asking them to find each feature, and to suggest what they think they might have been used for.

Afterwards, pupils could try one or more of the following activities.

■ Look for evidence to show how the building was heated - stoke hole, boiler platform and hypocaust. Point out the gap around the edge of the floor in the hot dry room, over which box tiles were placed to allow hot air pass up through the walls. Why were the door jambs of the hot dry room made from stone instead of wood? (The heat would cause wood to dry out and warp.)

■ Look at the water channels. Where do they come from and where do they lead? Follow the course of gutters and drains down to the latrines and out of the building. This is best observed from the bank opposite the latrines. Discuss why all waste water leads to the latrines (to flush them out.)

■ Help pupils understand how the bathhouse was used by following the routine of a bather. Enter the changing room, visit the latrines, and then return to the changing room for exercise. Have a quick cold bath to remove the surface dirt. Follow this by some time in the hot steam rooms to sweat out any ingrained dirt. Relax and socialise in the warm rooms before taking a hot bath and spending some time in the hot dry rooms. Finally cool off in the cold plunge and then get dressed.

■ Ask pupils to imagine the building with higher walls, a roof and small windows high up. What might the interior have looked like? What might they see, hear or smell. Compare with pupils' own experiences of bathing.

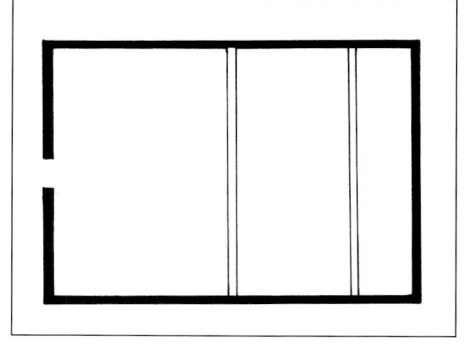

Plan of the headquarters building.

Headquarters building

As this building has a clearly-defined layout you can use it for a simple surveying and planning activity.

Give pupils an outline plan divided into the three main areas (see above) and ask them to locate and draw the main features in each.

■ In the courtyard, look for the well, the gutters, and the columns for the covered walkway and the entrances.

■ In the cross-hall, look for the pillars that supported the roof, the exits and the tribunal (raised platform from where the commanding officer addressed his officers and administered justice).

■ In the suite of offices, look for the dividing walls of each room, the military shrine and the steps down to the strong room.

Artist's impression of the bathhouse at Chesters.   RIGHT: Plan of the bathhouse.

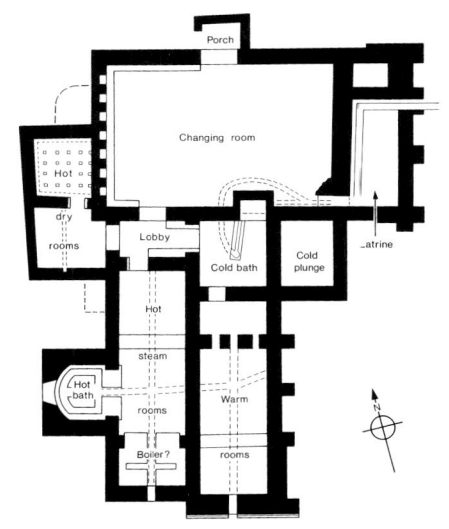

Role-play activities

These are short, simple activities which give a context for exploring buildings and to help pupils work out how they were used. They do not require skills in drama, nor do they require extensive knowledge of the site. All you need do is to explain briefly what the building is, and through simple role-play, pupils can expand on how they were used and to imagine what life might have been like.

Returning to camp

You or your helpers could lead groups of pupils around the site in the role of soldiers returning to the fort after a mission. Begin your walk by approaching a gateway, then passing through it. The first point of call might be to report to the headquarters building, then on to the centurion's house before returning to the barracks. Afterwards they might go to the baths (at Chesters) or into the vicus (Housesteads). Give each pupil a plan with the route marked out for them to follow. At each building ask pupils to describe what the soldier might see or hear, and then suggest what he might feel or think. Pupils' responses could be recorded in boxes around the edge of the plan. A similar route could be developed at Corbridge, using the fountain house, temple, barracks, officer's house and forum building.

Marching out

Organise your class into a troop setting out in formation on a long march. At Chesters or Housesteads you could begin either at the headquarters building or in the space between the barrack blocks. Set off through the fort, marching down the streets and out through a gateway. At Corbridge you could assemble your class in the road between the compounds and march along the Stanegate. Discuss with pupils how many troops can fit across the road; what might it sound like; how they might feel and how people might react to see a large group of armoured soldiers marching towards them.

Guarding the fort

At Chesters or Housesteads send small groups of pupils with a helper to each of the gateways and pretend to be soldiers on guard duty. Get them to work out where each soldier might stand, bearing in mind that the gateway would have been two storeys high (give helpers photocopies of drawings from this book to help them visualise the gateway). First, look at the remains and work out how many gates there were and how they operated. Then consider what they would do when visitors approached, or how would they react if an enemy attacked.

Moving on

In small groups stand around an artist's impression and ask pupils to choose one of the characters in the scene. Describe what is in front, behind, above, to the right and left of them. Discuss what might they hear or smell; who is next to them? What would it feel like to be there, and what might that person be thinking? Then get pupils to stand in the exact place of that person and 'unfreeze' the scene. Continue the action for 15 seconds asking pupils what that character might be doing. Freeze and ask pupils to describe what that person would see now, this time without referring to the artist's impression.

Site newspaper

Pupils could create a newspaper for the site in the second century AD. It could contain articles, features, adverts, letters or fort commands. Begin in school by looking at the content and layout of newsletters (if available look at some of the commercially-produced books for children in this style). Explore and explain different forms of language. Discuss possible suggestions for articles in the newspaper and assign them to pairs or small groups of pupils to investigate during the visit. Draft notes on site, and refine them on your return to school, adding a suitable headline. Agree which features require a supporting image.

Language and literacy

A visit to Hadrian's Wall or the sites along it is particularly atmospheric, providing a stimulus for creative writing. This experience will also support historical investigation by offering different ways for pupils to present their findings and to write for different purposes. The activities below offer an alternative focus for your visit.

Promoting the Wall

Ask pupils to work in groups to design posters or press adverts that encourage people to visit the site or the Wall itself. This could be an ICT project, involving persuasive writing. Discuss beforehand the layout and structure of an advert. Identify different forms of text - strapline, description, captions or directions. Look at why different sizes of print are used, the length of sentences and their content. What type of vocabulary is used and why? During your visit walk around the site asking each group to identify parts that they could photograph which might encourage people to make a visit. As soon as they have taken each photograph pupils should write a caption for it. Back at school ask each group to design their advert or poster, selecting only three images and captions. They also need to create a strapline for the top of the advert and summarise the site in twenty words. Plan with them where to use persuasive or descriptive language, and when to use large or small text.

Informing the visitor

Pupils can work as a class to produce an information leaflet for the site. During your visit divide your class into smaller groups, giving each a different building and ask them to compile a list of words or sentences to describe it. These will be used back at school to draft a fuller description. Also on site ask them to decide upon two photographs of the building, one a general view, and the other of a significant detail. On your return to school agree an overall scheme or layout for the leaflet and allot each group an amount of space for the information about their building. The leaflet could be designed using ICT or by a cut and paste technique.

Alternatively, pupils could work in groups to produce an interpretation panel, which could explain their building to younger children. Written information can be supported with photographs and scanned images.

Living on the frontier

Use pupils' feelings and observations which they recorded during familiarisation activities to imagine themselves as:

- a newly-recruited soldier on his first day on guard duty on the Wall or at one of the gates at Chesters or Housesteads
- the wife of a soldier recently posted to the Wall from another part of Britain and now lives in the civilian settlement at Housesteads, or the wife of a commanding officer who has recently arrived at her new home at Chesters
- a child living at Corbridge town.

Show photographs or slides to remind pupils of their visit, then discuss how each character might feel about living or working in that place. Pupils could present this by drafting a letter that each person might have sent to a friend, either in Rome or in Britain.

Roman Wall Blues

The wind whistles past the cool grey stone,
I'm a lonely soldier, all on my own.

The freezing rain trickles down my neck,
I'm cold, starving, a nervous wreck.

I kneel down and pray for Rome,
But Rome is gone, I have no home.

I'm sick and tired of the old stone wall,
But it still towers over me, proud and tall.

As I hobble along cold and bored,
I think of the rich Emperor... My Lord.

I look to the future and only see war,
I see my fate, me... no more.

Seventy-three miles

Along the wet winding wall,
The weary soldiers crawl,

They live and work and fight together
In every dreary weather,

Summer and spring bring sun, wind and rain,
Autumn and winter bring nothing but pain,

Emperor Hadrian is building a wall
To keep out the strangers, Scots and all.

Starting in the west at Port Carlisle,
It grew inch by inch in Roman style,

Seventy-three miles of blood, sweat and tears,
Hundreds of years of hopes and fears,

Finally arriving in the east,
The soldiers had completed this fantastic feat.

Bibliography and Resources

Roman Britain
Alcock, J, *Life in Roman Britain*, English Heritage/Batsford, 1996, ISBN 0-7134-6745-2.
McAleavey, T, *Life in Roman Britain*, English Heritage, 1999, ISBN 1-85074-733-4.
Salway, P, *The Oxford Illustrated History of Roman Britain*, Oxford University Press, 1993, ISBN 0-19-822984-4.

Army and forts
Bédoyére, G de la, *Hadrian's Wall*, Tempus, 1998, ISBN 0-7524-1407-0
Bidwell, P, *Roman Forts in Britain*, English Heritage/Batsford, 1997, ISBN 0-7134-7100-X
Breeze, D.J, *Roman Forts in Britain*, Shire, 1983, ISBN 0-85263-654-7

Educational approaches
Barnes, J, *A Teacher's Guide to Design & Technology and the Historic Environment*, English Heritage, 1999, ISBN 1-85074-1.
Copeland, T, *A Teacher's Guide to Geography and the Historic Environment*, English Heritage, 1993, ISBN 1-85074-332-0.
Copeland, T, *A Teacher's Guide to Maths and the Historic Environment*, English Heritage, 1992, ISBN 1-85074-329-0.
Durbin, G, Morris, S, & Wilkinson, S, *A Teacher's Guide to Learning from Objects*, English Heritage, 1990, ISBN 1-85074-259-6.
Lockey, M, & Walmsley, D, *A Teacher's Guide to Art and the Historic Environment*, English Heritage, 1999, ISBN 1-85074-651-6.
Pownall, J, & Hutson, N, *A Teacher's Guide to Science and the Historic Environment*, English Heritage, 1992, 1-85074-331-2.
Watson, I, *Using Roman Sites*, English Heritage, 1997, ISBN 1-85074-334-7.
Wheatley, G, *World Heritage Sites*, English Heritage, 1997, ISBN 1-85074-446-7.

Maps
Roman Britain, historical map and guide, Ordnance Survey, ISBN 0-319-29029-8.

Aerial photographs
These are available from the National Monuments Record Centre, Kemble Drive, Swindon, SN2 2GZ. Tel 01793 414600. E-mail nmrinfo@english-heritage.org.uk

Poster Packs
Hadrian's Wall, English Heritage, 2002, ISBN 1-85074-811-X. Contains aerial photographs and artists' impressions to give a fuller picture of the different elements of Hadrian's Wall and its impact on the area. Includes an 8-page teacher's information booklet.
Roman Britain, English Heritage, 1997, ISBN 1-85074-684-2. Contains eight A3 posters.
Interpreting the past, English Heritage, 1999, ISBN 1-85074-737-7. Contains six colour posters with 8-page booklet with activities to help teachers use artists' impressions on site and in the classroom.
Time Detectives, English Heritage, 2002, ISBN 1-85074-778-4. Contains six A3 posters with 8-page teacher booklet with curriculum ideas.

CD-ROM
Real Romans, English Heritage/TAG, 1999, ISBN 1-902604-00-7. Includes 48-page book.

Videos
Talkin' Roman, English Heritage, 1996, 20 mins. Suitability: Key Stage 2. Investigates life in Britain under the Romans using characters from the past.
Hadrian's Wall - A journey back in time, 1998, 48 mins. (Available from English Heritage)

English Heritage is the national leader in heritage education. It aims to help teachers at all levels to use the resource of the historic environment. Each year it welcomes over half a million pupils, students and teachers on free educational group visits to over 400 historic sites in its care. For free copies of the *Free Educational Visits* booklets, the *Resources* catalogue, and *Heritage Learning*, our termly magazine, contact:
English Heritage Education
Freepost 22 (WD214)
London W1E 7EZ
Tel. 020-7973 3442
Fax. 020-7973 3443
www.HeritageEducation.net

HADRIAN'S WALL
WORLD HERITAGE SITE

one NorthEast
The Development Agency for the North East of England

Acknowledgements
The design and printing of this handbook is partly financed by Hadrian's Wall Tourism Partnership and One NorthEast. Scheme of work on pages 30-31 was devised in consultation with members of Hadrian's Wall Education Forum.
Descriptions of the forts at South Shields, Birdoswald, Segedunum and Vindolanda were supplied by each site.

Opposite: How the headquarters building at Housesteads might have looked in the third century.
Back cover: The Wall under construction.